The Birth That's Right for You

A Doctor and a Doula

Help You Choose and Customize

the Best Birth Option to Fit Your Needs

AMEN NESS, M.D.

LISA GOULD RUBIN, CD, CCE

JACKIE FREDERICK-BERNER

McGraw·Hill

New York   Chicago   San Francisco   Lisbon   London   Madrid   Mexico City
Milan   New Delhi   San Juan   Seoul   Singapore   Sydney   Toronto

The *McGraw·Hill* Companies

Library of Congress Cataloging-in-Publication Data

Ness, Amen.
    The birth that's right for you : a doctor and a doula help you choose and customize
the best birth option to fit your needs / by Amen Ness, Lisa Gould Rubin, Jackie
Frederick-Berner.—1st ed.
       p.   cm.
    ISBN 0-07-145963-4 (alk. paper)
     1. Childbirth—Popular works.   2. Labor (Obstetrics)—Popular works.
3. Delivery (Obstetrics)—Popular works.   I. Rubin, Lisa Gould.   II. Frederick-
Berner, Jackie.   III. Title.

RG652.N47   2006
618.4—dc22   2005015887

1 2 3 4 5 6 7 8 9 0   DOC/DOC   0 9 8 7 6 5

ISBN 0-07-145963-4

McGraw-Hill books are available at special quantity discounts to use as premiums and
sales promotions, or for use in corporate training programs. For more information, please
write to the Director of Special Sales, Professional Publishing, McGraw-Hill, Two Penn
Plaza, New York, NY 10121-2298. Or contact your local bookstore.

None of the information in this book is intended as a substitute for qualified advice from a
licensed doctor, midwife, or doula. The authors and publisher disclaim any liability arising
directly or indirectly from the use of this book.

The stories in this book are true, but the names have been changed.

For my partners, who helped and supported me during seventeen years of practice.

For my patients, who help me see all the different ways women give birth and the unique rhythms of every birth.

And for Jocelyn, Tehila, Adina, and Brit.

—*A. N.*

For my mother, who taught me so well to be my own best friend that when she said, "Nothing should be delivered at home except for the New York Times," *I went ahead and had two home births anyway.*

For my daughters, Indiana, Hallie, and Liberty, whose births transformed me and gave me the honor of being their mother.

And for Peter, my husband, whose love is a constant reminder that dreams really do come true.

—*L. G. R.*

For Benjamin and Theo, whose births inspired the writing of this book and forever inspire my life.

For my family, who supports me with all their hearts.

And for Paul, who loves me with all his.

—*J. F.-B.*

Contents

Acknowledgments

A Heartfelt Thank-You

The birth of this book would not have been possible without the following people, and for you we are eternally grateful.

All the women whose births we've had the honor and good fortune to be present at and all those who generously shared their birth stories with us so we, in turn, could share them with you.

Jessica Papin, agent in absentia, who believed in us from conception.

John Aherne, our editor, who knew that this book needed to be published (and in doing so, learned more about childbirth than—at times—he ever wanted to know!).

Introduction

This is not a book about being pregnant. We're not here to tell you about eating for two, where to find that miracle stretch-mark cream (there just isn't one), or that in your fourth month your baby might be sucking his or her little thumb. By now it's no secret that you can find volume after volume on these very subjects, covering everything you might be doing, feeling, questioning, and wondering during your nine months of growing your baby. This book is different. This book is about what happens at the end of those nine months when you have to give birth to that baby.

If you're newly pregnant, you're probably thinking a book about giving birth is the last thing you need. Your mind is very much in the present, perhaps wondering, "How am I going to get through yet another day, and accomplish everything that I need to accomplish, when I feel like I'm going to throw up before I even open my eyes and, once I do pry them open, they're ready to close by noon?" If you're one of those women lucky enough not to be experiencing morning sickness, you may doubt whether you even *are* pregnant, let alone that you'll eventually give birth. And if you've had a tough time *getting* and/or *staying* pregnant, your focus is on keeping what you've worked and hoped so hard for.

But one day you feel it—a faint fluttering or tapping like Morse code inside your body signaling, "I'm here." Then as your belly (and everything else) expands over the weeks and months ahead, that faint fluttering gives way to a kicking, somersaulting, hiccupping little being. And sooner or later it hits you. There is no turning back. Those countless pregnancy questions are swiftly replaced by one large, looming one: "How am I going to get this baby out of my body?"

Now, odds are, ever since you announced your pregnancy, you've been barraged with birth stories. Your mother's. Your sister's. Your best friend's. Your not-so-best friend's. Even people you hardly know are telling you what it was like for them *and* what you should do. There's the cousin who moaned and chanted her way through each contraction, delivered her baby in a squatting position with family and friends by her side, and went home from the birth center that day. There's the mother-in-law who was completely knocked out during the birth of her babies. There's the friend who labored at home for as long as she could and was eight centimeters by the time she got to the hospital. There's the coworker who scheduled a cesarean delivery so her baby would be born before the holidays. For as many women as there are having babies, there are as many different stories. And it's with all these stories swirling around in your head, along with your own ideas and feelings about childbirth, that you set out to figure out how *you* would like to give birth.

So you hit the books. Your options? The meager few that are devoted entirely to childbirth or the slim one or two chapters that conclude all those pregnancy books and seem almost like an afterthought—"OK, time to wrap it up. Let's get the baby out!" You ask your doctor or midwife about the different kinds of childbirth classes out there. You ask your friends what they did. Or, you don't even ask. You just sign up for the class offered at the hospital where you're going to have your baby.

But before you go any further, we need to warn you about something. We think every single one of those books, childbirth classes, and well-meaning advisers should come with a disclaimer that says something like "the opinions presented here are the sole reflection of the opinion-giver and may very well *not be applicable* to the receiver." Because every birth book that you read and everything that you hear, whether from friends, family, your childbirth instructor, or complete strangers, is based on one thing and one thing only: how *they* think women should be having babies. It's not about you.

It's about what worked for them. Or, didn't work. It's about what-ever birthing philosophy they happen to adhere to. Or, don't adhere to. As passionately as they paint the picture of the "perfect birth," it's only "perfect" because it worked for them. They really have no idea what will work for *you*. How could they?

And for that matter, how do you know what will work for you? What if you don't even know what you want? How do you prepare for an entirely unknown, potentially stressful, and painful experience at the end of which you're handed a baby and your life as you know it is changed forever? That's why we're here. This book is designed to help you figure that all out.

> You already have what it takes to have a good and sat-isfying birth experience!

Contrary to popular belief, you don't have to embark on a huge research project to find the answers you need. Forget about learning some strange breathing technique or committing to memory those textbook illustrations of pushing positions. Believe it or not, you already have what it takes to have a good and satisfying birth expe-rience! The very same things that you have been relying on all your life when you're anxious, stressed out, or in pain are the ones that will get you through labor and delivery.

Unlike all those childbirth books and classes out there, we're not going to teach you a particular method or some newfangled child-birth technique, because unless they happen to be *exactly* what you need when you're feeling anxious, in pain, or afraid, they just won't work. In fact, they'll work against you. Why? Because you're smack-dab in the middle of labor and attempting to get through it with something you'd never do in the first place.

That's why you're bound to hear during your pregnancy if you haven't already: "Oh, you're taking Lamaze class [feel free to substitute any other 'method' for that matter]. It doesn't work." It clearly didn't for her. Because inevitably, when you get to that point in labor where you're maxed out, any strategies except for the ones that come naturally to you will fall by the wayside. It's really just basic human nature. You don't turn into a completely different person in labor and delivery. Under pressure, you rely on what's already in place, what you've been doing all these years.

> Our method is *your* method. Instead of trying to fit you into a system that doesn't take into account the kind of person you are, we'll show you how you can have a labor and delivery that does.

That is the crux of what this book is about. And that's what makes us entirely different from the Lamazes, the Bradleys, and any other childbirth method or book that you'll come across. Our method is *your* method. Instead of trying to fit you into a system that doesn't take into account the kind of person you are (which basically leaves it all up to chance), we'll show you how you can have a labor and delivery that does. We'll help you zero in on what exactly you do in your everyday life to feel better. Then we'll show you how those same comfort measures will help you in childbirth. For instance, if you get through your period by popping ibuprofen every four hours or you can't have a cavity filled without getting gas, pain relief in labor may very likely be your best friend. If you tend to unwind after a hard day by climbing into a warm bath, that could provide instant relief and relaxation in labor. If it's your habit to move around when you're feeling anxious or in pain, then rocking in a rocking chair or swaying back and forth on a birth ball could make all the difference in the world to you.

Just as you make choices in your life that reflect the kind of person you are, we'll show you how you can depend on that same decision-making process when it comes to having a baby. It's a good bet that the things in your life that are most satisfying and truly meet your needs—whether it's where you live, the kind of work you do, the way you socialize, a hobby, a vacation spot, or a physical or mental pursuit—are accurate indicators of your true nature. Do you thrive in the hustle and bustle of a city or prefer a more rural setting? Does being in a group of people energize you or do you do better one-on-one? We'll show you how being sensitive to these seemingly little bits of information about yourself can have a major impact on your birth experience. It can mean the difference between, for example, where you decide to have your baby or whether having your partner, mother, sisters, *and* best friend in attendance at your birth will help you feel safe and supported or drive you up the wall.

The reason this works is really quite simple: by identifying beforehand these different things about yourself, you'll go into labor knowing specifically what you need and how to get those needs met. *And that's what makes all the difference in the world.* Because if your needs are being met—no matter what they are—and if you're doing what you naturally do—no matter what that is—you're going to feel good about what's happening. That's not to say it'll be "pain-free," "perfect," "not messy," and so on. But in the midst of everything that your labor entails, you're far more likely to feel safe and secure when your needs are being taken care of and your wishes respected. When you feel that way, your labor just goes better. Period. And even if things happen differently than you imagined or hoped, if the choices you make along the way are in sync with your needs and desires, you'll wind up feeling satisfied with your birth experience.

Now, for some of you that means coming into labor and delivery with your veins exposed, saying, "Give me everything you've got. Just make this pain go away." For others of you it's breathing, rocking, and moaning through each contraction without the slightest intervention. Obviously there are a myriad of scenarios between the two, because everyone handles labor differently based on their individual personalities and needs. This book will help you figure out what you need and show you just how to get those needs met. We'll take you through the experience of childbirth and, through a series of critical steps, help you identify the choices that fit you best—from who will deliver your baby to where and how you'd like your baby to be born.

We'll help you take a look at your expectations. Because the very first step to getting clear on what will work for you in labor and delivery is to peel away all those nagging expectations that really aren't your own, that come from what you're hearing or reading. And we'll help you identify and cut through any pressure you might be putting on yourself to be someone you're not—"stronger, less fearful, happier"—so you can be exactly who you are in labor and delivery.

> The best and most satisfying birth experiences happen when you're able to make choices in labor and delivery that are based on who you are, not someone some childbirth expert tells you that you should be.

We'll help you ascertain if your doctor or midwife is the right one for you and, if not, help you pick one who is.

We'll help you figure out where you'll feel most comfortable laboring and the people you'll want by your side.

We'll help you identify how you deal with pain and stress in your everyday life and show you how these very same coping strategies, or variations of them, will help you during each stage of labor.

We'll help you take a realistic look at yourself so you can get a feel for whether or not you'll need pain medication and, if so, what would work best for you.

We'll help you understand what you might be feeling or fearing on the brink of delivery. And that birth is not just about what's happening for you. It's also about what's happening for your baby. His or her position or well-being will also impact the way your birth goes.

Finally, we'll help you become aware of the range of emotions you might be feeling after giving birth—from falling in love with your baby at first sight (or not) to needing some time for yourself to decompress from the experience.

Our job is to help you come away with a birth experience that is a custom fit for you, because we believe that when it comes to the birth of your baby, you are the expert. The best and most satisfying birth experiences happen when you're able to make choices in labor and delivery that are based on who you are, not someone some childbirth expert tells you that you should be.

In the following chapters, we'll help you tap into the unique combination of all those things that make you who you are. And we'll show you how you can use that information about yourself as a reference point when deciding what will work best for you in childbirth. It's really very simple: always referring back to you will lead you to the birth that's right for you. And we'll help you get there.

· 1 ·

Having Babies:
Then and Now

If being exactly who you are is exactly the way to have a good and satisfying birth experience, how did we get to this point in time where it is a concept that sounds like—and really *is*—a revolutionary idea?

Childbirth Through the Years

Up until the 1900s babies were born at home with the help of a midwife. There were no epidurals, no emergency cesareans, no neonatal teams waiting in the wings. Instead, women relied on the reassuring presence and hands-on approach of their midwives, female family members, and friends to help bring their babies into the world. These early midwives were with the laboring mother every step of the way—guiding, supporting, and nurturing her.

Enter the age of science and doctors with their medical bags containing ether anesthesia and drugs to stop hemorrhaging and infection. Promised painless, safer births, women signed on in droves. By the 1940s, hospital births became the norm and for the next two decades women basically "slept" through childbirth.

By the time the 1960s rolled around, the alarm went off and women woke up with some serious doubts about the sanitized, industrial, and, at times, humiliating process that childbirth had become. They didn't want to go through labor alone or with Nurse Ratched. They didn't want to be shaved, strapped down, and rendered unconscious during childbirth only to find out hours later whether they had a son or a daughter.

So they set out to create a better way—one that combined the nurturing and supportive aspects of the early home births with the medical advances of the time. Many women wanted to be present for the births of their babies. They wanted to make their own decisions about whether or not they needed pain relief. They wanted to feel safe and supported through labor. They wanted their partners with them. *They wanted a say in what happened to them and their babies.*

Getting doctors and hospitals to change what they'd been doing was a slow and sometimes adversarial process. The arrival of the fetal monitor and skyrocketing malpractice lawsuits led to a standoff between doctors and patients. To protect themselves from being sued, doctors began to practice defensive obstetrics, relying on fetal monitors and interventions such as cesareans to ensure a "healthy outcome." Women and their partners, adamant about not having high-tech birth experiences, began to practice defensive childbirth. They were fueled by the childbirth education movement, the purpose of which was to empower women to make informed choices. Women were instructed to arm themselves with birth plans that demanded "no fetal monitoring, no IVs, no episiotomies, no cesarean deliveries" but also commanded "deliver us a perfect baby." At the same time, *women* were dividing against each other into camps of "natural" versus medicated childbirth, throwing stones of judgment and guilt at each other.

Changing the Face of Childbirth

From the 1960s through the next approximately thirty years, the winds of change kicked up many emotionally charged storms. Doctors and patients were at odds with each other. Women were at odds with each other. Spouses and partners were thrust into the role of medical consultant, lawyer, police officer, and support system all rolled into one. But with these storms came real change. The wants and needs of women slowly but surely changed the face of childbirth.

Except now, instead of the medical establishment telling us how we should be having babies, we have childbirth experts saying what they think is best. Lamaze: *A world of confident women choosing normal birth. Normal* according to whom? What happens if your definition of normal doesn't match up? The Bradley Method: *Husband-coached, natural childbirth* promoting a 90 percent "success rate" for unmedicated births. But maybe your partner is not such a natural in the birthing room. And if you take twelve weeks of Bradley classes and end up using medication, does that make you feel like you failed somehow? Birth Works: *Every woman inherently knows how to give birth.* That might not ring true for you, especially if you've never even *held* a baby in your arms, let alone given birth to one. Hypno-Birthing: *Pain-free labor through self-hypnosis.* Pain-free sounds pretty appealing. But maybe you're the type who finds it difficult to visualize anything other than what is actually happening.

These messages may be subtly couched in the pages of a book, or not so subtly flashed from a website, but the point is always the same: *We* know best. *We* have the studies to prove it. And *we'll* show you how to do it *our* way. For along with these "methods" comes the work—philosophies to buy into, ideals to adhere to, responsibilities to live up to, and techniques and strategies to learn and practice.

So where does that leave you? Unfortunately, having a baby has turned into a very big test. Your assignment? Diligently learn all sorts of new behaviors and ideas that may not have anything to do with who you are. And once you're in labor, should you happen to need something outside the margins of the method you've chosen or, if your birth unfolds in a different way than the method prescribes, then somehow you've failed. Sadly enough, the test scorers aren't just the "birth experts." They're your friends, family, coworkers, and even the checkout clerk at the supermarket. And your toughest grader may very well be yourself.

Now in everybody's defense, childbirth is something that evokes a lot of passion. The birth of a baby is miraculous and life-changing. Many people who have had amazing, deeply touching experiences want to help others have the same. For some, including those who fought so hard for change, it becomes a mission. And while their intentions are good (well, almost always good), they're missing one crucial point. Everyone is different. What may work brilliantly for one person can be a disaster for someone else.

Writing a New Chapter

We'd like to think of this approach as the next revolutionary chapter in childbirth. Simply stated, it's OK just to be yourself during the birth of your baby. In fact, it's more than OK, it's crucial. It's what leads you to a good and satisfying birth. It's not about creating a "new and improved" version of you. You're fine just the way you are. It's simply a matter of understanding how what you do already to handle stress, anxiety, and pain will look during labor and delivery and how that will help you through the experience.

> It's OK just to be yourself during the birth of your baby. In fact, it's more than OK, it's crucial.

That's not to say you'll throw out the window all the methods and ideas that you've been hearing and reading about. You might end up taking some ideas from one method and some from another (kind of like choosing one from column "A" and one from column

"B" on a Chinese menu), or you might decide that one method is a perfect fit for you. But rather than signing on blindly and possibly feeling inadequate at the other end, you'll choose something because it's a natural extension of who you are—it matches up to *you* rather than you trying to fit yourself into *it*, like Cinderella's slipper.

> The ultimate goal is that you come through your birth experience feeling good about yourself.

There will always be something to fight for when it comes to childbirth. Change is a necessary part of life. But there is one thing that never changes. You are, and you will always be, your own best expert. Despite what you're hearing from friends and family. Despite what all those experts may be saying. And even despite all the research and studies they may be waving in your face. For every opinion and bit of research that supports one point of view, you can always find someone who or something else that supports just the opposite view.

You'll figure it out the way you naturally do. Maybe you'll talk to your doctor or midwife, sift through whatever information you need to, or run your choices by the people you trust. But, ultimately, you'll be your own personal sounding board when it comes to knowing what's right for you. "I want my baby delivered by a midwife in a free-standing birth center in a comfy room with a four-poster bed." "I want to be induced and then I want an epidural. I want my husband, my mother, and my doula by my side." "I don't want an epidural, and I'm going to labor at home for as long as I can. I'm packing CDs, my own pillows, and my blanket for when I get to the hospital." "I'm scheduling a cesarean delivery, and I want to stay in the hospital for as long as my insurance lets me." In the end, *you're* the one who needs to be comfortable with any decision you make.

As much as the experts would probably disagree, there's really no one right way to have a baby. In addition to a healthy mother and healthy baby, we believe the ultimate goal is that you come through your birth experience feeling good about yourself. And this happens most often when there is tolerance and support for all the ways women want and need to give birth.

In this book, while we touch on births that take place at a birth center and at home, we take you through a hospital birth because that's how the majority of women in this country choose to give birth. But no matter where you have your baby, the principles we outline are universal. They can be applied to every birth, because it's not only about the choices themselves, it's about helping you make the choices that are *right for you*.

· 2 ·

The Birth
That's Right for You

So where do you start? Right where you are. Everyone comes to pregnancy and childbirth at all different stages of readiness and awareness. You might not have a clue about what to ask or even where to begin. Or, maybe you've read every book, magazine article, and study you can get your hands on. Whatever the case, it's a sure bet you're getting advice and hearing stories from those around you, and what eventually happens is that you start "trying it all on."

While reading a pregnancy magazine, you come across a photo of a beautiful woman surrounded by glowing candles, blissfully breathing through a contraction. The person who cuts your hair tells you that she has no intention of feeling anything. She's getting an epidural as soon as she gets to the hospital. Then, whether you're even aware of it or not, you form a mental picture of yourself in these different situations to see how they might feel for you. Your reactions could range from "#★! No!" to "Yes, where do I sign up?!" to "I wish I could be the kind of person who would do that."

When something feels absolutely right or absolutely wrong, there's usually no denying it. But when you're feeling "not so sure" or "unsettled" about something, it's worth taking a closer look. If you find yourself wishing you could be "stronger, braver, and so on," maybe that's a warning sign. It almost always means that your expectations are unrealistic or unfair to you or you're making somebody else's expectations your own.

Expecting Realistically: How Your Expectations Shape Your Birth Experience

In the following chapters, we'll delve into all your childbirth choices, including the person you want to deliver your baby, where you want to give birth, how you see yourself giving birth, and who you want with you. But before going through those choices, we'd like to take a moment to introduce you in this chapter to the part of yourself that will influence every single decision you make. Yes, every last one. Say hello to your expectations. They come in four varieties:

- The ones that truly reflect you
- The ones that are everyone else's
- The ones that you think you should have (including the "shoulds" that are masking what you're afraid of)
- The ones that don't take into account that things might go differently than you expect

When you make decisions that come from expectations that are authentically your own, you're paving the way toward the birth that's right for you. But when you make decisions based on expectations that don't accurately represent your personality, you're veering off-track. And guess what? Having unrealistic expectations may very well be the biggest cause of all the childbirth "horror" (translation—terribly disappointing) stories you've heard.

For example, you're entertaining the thought of a water birth because your sister had one and it was amazing and now she says you've got to do it, too. You think you want to, but you keep flip-flopping over the idea. You're not the type to take long soaks in the tub. When push comes to shove, you'd rather hang out on the beach than swim in the ocean. You keep remembering that scary time as a kid when you were just learning to swim and you started to go under.

As you go back and forth trying to come to a decision, there's one important constant in all of this. When you go into childbirth with a realistic picture of who you are and what you need to feel safe, less anxious, taken care of, respected—whatever it is that's important to you—you've done everything within your power to set yourself up for a good birth experience. And as you've probably guessed, in this case, choosing a water birth isn't going to do that. It just doesn't come naturally to you. In fact, it's the equivalent of forcing yourself to jump through a ring of fire. So tell your sister that, while you're thrilled to death for her that she had such a great birth, a water birth just isn't for you. You don't even like water. Or don't tell her anything. Just make sure you throw that water birth idea out with the bathwater.

> When you make decisions that come from expectations that are authentically your own, you're paving the way toward the birth that's right for you.

By now, you've probably already made some choices about what you want in childbirth. You may have some very strong feelings about those choices. Or maybe they're just inklings. Wherever you are in the process, we'll show you how to clarify which choices are driven by expectations that accurately represent your personality and which aren't. When you look at your options through the lens of your expectations, three things will happen: (1) you'll know whether the option is really based on your own expectations—instead of everyone else's; (2) you'll find out whether it's about who *you* are, not who you think you *should* be; and (3) you'll see if what you've chosen leaves room for the possibility that things might not go exactly as you hope they will.

Your Expectations, Not Theirs

Your friends, coworkers, and family who've had babies have lots of ideas on the "best" way to have a baby, and they've probably been eagerly sharing these ideas with you every chance they get. Yes, they all mean well (most of the time). But their thoughts and advice are based on what *they* went through in childbirth—an experience unique to them.

> If you're feeling the least bit uncomfortable with what you're hearing, there's a very good possibility that it is not really right for you. The best method for you in labor and delivery is always your own.

Maybe you're hearing things like, "Are you crazy? Just get the epidural." Or, "Don't have an epidural, you'll wind up with a C-section." When how you see yourself having your baby matches what you're hearing, you're going to feel very supported. When it doesn't, you could end up feeling anxious and full of doubt about your own decisions. And when you're not really sure about how you feel, you might feel pressure to do something that's not right for you.

Kate: I was at the point where it was time to start thinking about child-birth classes. I had pretty much decided to sign up for a class that my best friend, who had just had her baby, couldn't stop raving about and was pushing me to take. She spent most of her labor either in the shower or being massaged, gave birth without drugs, and said it was such an amazing experience that maybe she'd give birth at home next time. I could never imagine having my baby at home. I wasn't even sure if I could make it through labor without pain medication. But I wanted my birth to be as great as hers. So as my due date got closer and closer and I still wasn't enrolled in a class, I got nervous and figured I should just sign up for the class that she took.

When someone you really like and trust is advising you to do something you're not so sure about, it can be a challenge to figure out where you stand. Think about it. You're in a vulnerable position because you don't have the experience she has—giving birth is, as of yet, an unknown to you. And if someone you're close to is over the moon about something that unequivocally worked for her, you're naturally going to pay attention. But pay attention to yourself. If you're feeling the least bit uncomfortable with what you're hearing, there's a very good possibility that it is not really right for you. The best method for you in labor and delivery is always your own.

Finding *Your* Method

The first step when you discover yourself in this very common situation is to cut yourself some slack. You don't know exactly what you're going to need during childbirth. How could you? You've never done this before! And even if you have, every labor and delivery is different.

- Take pause. Get some mental distance from the fact that this worked for your best friend. Do whatever you usually do to try to get some perspective. Take a walk, go shopping, breathe, exercise, meditate, get your nails done. If you need a sounding board, talk to someone you trust who can be objective.
- "Try on" the birth option that you're considering to really feel how it sits with you. And ask yourself some questions that will help you get to the core of how you really feel. For example, in the above scenario Kate could ask herself: *What*

do I typically do when I'm in pain? Do I curl up into a ball in my bed? Do I pace around? Do I moan and yell? Do I "tough" it out? Do I lose it when it gets to be too much? *How do I feel about pain medication for labor and delivery?* Am I absolutely sure that I *do* or *don't* want it? Am I on the fence? Do I want to wait and see how I feel once I'm in labor?

- See how your answers match up with the birth option you're trying on. It may be a direct hit. It may be that parts of it feel right to you and you'll be able to modify the rest to fit your needs. Or, your answers may tell you that it's not a good match but bring you closer to what is.

■ The Good Birth Match

Our many years of helping women have babies have led us to develop a pretty accurate way for you to see what kinds of coping strategies will work best for you in labor. We call it The Good Birth Match. What it does is help connect you—the type of person you are—to the kinds of labor coping strategies that fit you best. See which habits describe you in order to see how who you are matches up to what you might be doing in labor. As we've said before, how you deal with stress, anxiety, and pain in your day-to-day life will pretty much be the same in labor. That's why having a realistic picture of the strategies that you naturally use will help you have a realistic idea of the kind of birth that's right for you.

What do you do or need when you're stressed out, anxious, or in pain?	Here's how that might look in labor.
You head straight for the medicine cabinet at the first twinge of pain.	You get pain medication to take the edge off contractions and/or an epidural for complete pain relief.

You avoid traditional medicine and use alternatives such as homeopathy, herbs, acupuncture/acupressure, or chiropractic.

You use nondrug coping strategies such as alternating labor positions, getting in water (the shower or tub), massage, acupressure, breathing, or hypnosis—many of which we'll describe later on.

You start with alternatives; then move on to traditional medicine if you're not getting relief, i.e., Arnica first, Advil next.

You begin with the above nondrug coping strategies; then, if contractions get to be too much or your labor gets to be too long and you're exhausted, you get pain medication and/or an epidural.

You can't stay still and need to walk/pace, keep busy washing dishes or folding laundry, and so on.

You walk the well-worn path on the Labor & Delivery floor; rock in a rocking chair (borrow one from the newborn nursery or patient lounge if there isn't one in your room); move around on a birth ball (bring one with you); and sway your hips while standing and leaning over a stack of pillows on your raised bed, on all fours in bed, or in child's pose, and so on.

You climb into a bubble bath or sequester yourself in the shower.

You use the shower, tub, or Jacuzzi to cope with contractions and keep relaxed. (Bring your maternity bathing suit if you're modest and fresh clothes for your partner in case he or she gets

	sprayed.) You labor and give birth in a birthing pool. (See Chapter 4 for more on water births.)
You do an immediate wardrobe change, i.e., climb into a big, comfy shirt or sweats, put on your softest socks or slippers, wrap yourself in the robe you've had since high school, and so on.	You wear your own comfy clothes, such as a favorite oversized T-shirt, sweats, or yoga pants, instead of the hospital gown.
You watch/listen to the TV or music.	You have the TV on in your labor room (it might be on the entire time) or you bring a portable CD player so you can listen to your favorite music during different stages of your labor—whether you go from the sounds of the Brazilian rain forest to Beethoven to the Beatles.
You turn off all the lights and pull down the shades. Or, you need gentle daylight, the glow from a night-light ,or the flicker of TV in an otherwise dark room for comfort.	Your partner/spouse or doula learns where all the light switches are in order to create just the right atmosphere for you in your labor room. He or she could semiclose the curtains, turn off the room lights, and turn on the bathroom light and leave the bathroom door ajar. *Ahhh.*
You do lots of talking to burn off nervous energy.	You talk and your spouse or partner (or nurse, doula, doctor, etc.) listens and/or gives reassuring feedback from time to time.

You need quiet to stay centered.	Neither you nor your spouse or partner talk, except when necessary.
You tend to call your mother, sister, or best friend for feedback.	That person is with you at your birth providing the comfort and feedback you depend on.
You need physical connection.	You hold hands and/or your spouse/partner strokes your arm, pets your head, plays with your hair, or massages the usual places during or between contractions.
You need *not* to be touched. It's too much stimulation for you.	Your spouse/partner, nurse, and doula are aware and respectful of this and always ask first if touch is OK.

Kate: At my next prenatal visit I wound up asking my doctor about my friend's childbirth class. The more he described it, the more I realized that that wasn't really how I saw myself giving birth. We talked about what effects pain medication could have on my baby, and I realized I wasn't so opposed to an epidural. I'm now taking a class that's helping me figure out what I need in labor and delivery, including pain medication as an option. It's such a relief. I feel really good about the choices I'm making.

Kate was able to get something from her doctor that she couldn't possibly get from her best friend: an objective description of the childbirth class she was considering. That freed her to do the essential—look at the class through her own eyes instead of her friend's rose-colored glasses. Only then was she able to know if it was an honest fit. This seemingly small interaction between Kate and her doctor enabled her to take a huge step toward setting herself up for a birth that's right for her, not her best friend.

Who You Really Are, Not Who You Think You "Should" Be

Some unrealistic expectations come from what you're hearing or reading, but they can also come directly from you. This can happen if you're putting pressure on yourself to do something that doesn't feel right or to be someone you're not. For example, if you're the type who religiously plans and schedules every aspect of your life, the traditionally recommended "wait-and-see" approach to pain medication for labor and delivery might make you more than a little anxious. However, caught up in the pursuit to do what's "right," you might let those very real and valid feelings go unacknowledged and put pressure on yourself to be more flexible and "go with the flow." But in all fairness to you, "going with the flow" is really not a tack you would naturally take in your everyday life. It's just not who you are.

Here's the negative chain reaction that's set off by that kind of reasoning: by putting unfair demands on yourself, on some level, you're going to feel stressed, anxious, fearful, or a combination of all these emotions. Why? Because you're asking yourself to do something you wouldn't normally do. And when you carry this undue stress, anxiety, and fear into the labor and delivery room, those unsettling emotions can't help but affect your birth experience—the way things happen, or don't happen, and the way you feel about your experience during and after. If you're the type who has a hard time with a "wait-and-see" approach, all that unnecessary stress, anxiety, and fear could be eliminated by setting up beforehand, for example, the option of getting an epidural as close to your arrival at the hospital as possible. Or, conversely, getting the reassurance you may need that you won't be given or pressured into taking any medication without your consent. That's how you set yourself up for a positive chain reaction, because when you feel secure that your specific needs are being taken care of, the better your birth will go.

Quite frequently, the feeling that you "should" be *more* something (more open, more relaxed, or more fearless) is really masking what you're afraid of. For example, you're freaked out by hospitals but you've made up your mind that you're going to be brave. So "brave," in fact, that the thought of walking into one causes your jaw to immediately clench shut. Well, we must tell you it's pretty difficult to give birth to a baby with clenched teeth. (In fact, a relaxed jaw actually leads to a more relaxed cervix, which helps it to dilate.) While it might be hard for you to accept that you're afraid of something—whatever that may be—or even harder to begin to take a look at what's behind that fear, doing so is going to make for a better birth experience in the long run.

> *Jenny: When I was a little girl, my brother had horrible asthma attacks. A few times he was rushed to the hospital because he couldn't breathe. Since then, I've always been extremely anxious and uncomfortable in hospitals—the smells, the beeping monitors, the IVs. I can't even watch those kinds of shows on TV. Throughout my pregnancy I kept trying to ignore these feelings and convince myself I would be OK. Everything came to a head during my first childbirth class, which took place at the hospital where I was going to have my baby. I felt so panicky I don't know how I managed to sit through it.*

When it comes to having a baby, your fears can be pushed down for just so long. Since giving birth is a completely new experience that is very intense, it can't help but bring up stressful emotions and highlight your vulnerabilities. So even if your fears have managed to stay undercover throughout your pregnancy, it's pretty much a given that they'll emerge during labor and delivery in one form or another. For example, in the above scenario, if we were to play out

Jenny's discomfort with hospitals and incorporate what we know about the effects of fear on labor, left to its own devices that could translate into a "stalled" labor once she actually got to the hospital. She might then need Pitocin, the synthetic version of the body's hormone oxytocin, to jump-start her contractions. That, in turn, could lead to an epidural that Jenny really hadn't planned on or wanted. But by addressing her fear she could plan for the support she needed in any number of ways.

> The point is not to eradicate your fears but to figure out what you can do to provide for yourself whatever it is that will help you feel safe and supported.

Certain things about you can bring up fears about labor and delivery. While the anxiety and stress caused by these fears can vary in intensity, one thing is for certain: left unchecked they will have a direct effect on your birth experience. By getting a handle on your fears now, a runaway labor and delivery fueled by what you're afraid of can be derailed before the train ever leaves the station. Validating and understanding your fears is the first step toward easing them, because once you know what triggers them, you can begin to figure out strategies to reduce them.

Easing Your Fears

- Acknowledge them. The first step to working with your fears is to recognize them and try to get an idea where they're coming from.
- Go easy on yourself. Just like everything else you bring to the table, your fears are a valid part of you. You don't have to "suck it up" or be embarrassed by them. The point is not to

eradicate your fears but to figure out what you can do to provide for yourself whatever it is that will help you feel safe and supported, so they don't negatively affect your birth experience.

- Talk about your fears. Your doctor, midwife, doula, and/or childbirth instructor can help you understand what options you have during labor to reduce your anxiety. Keep exploring until you've come up with a plan that you're completely comfortable with. And if you feel like you're not getting the help you need from any one of them, seriously consider finding someone new.

- Talk to a therapist. There are certain experiences that can trigger intense, even debilitating fears: sexual abuse or rape, guilty feelings surrounding an abortion, miscarriage, a previous bad delivery experience, and exposure to traumatic labor stories are some. No matter what your fear, therapy can help and directly affect your labor and delivery for the better.

Jenny: After class, I asked my childbirth instructor, "If I'm so anxious about being in the hospital just for class, how am I going to survive being here to have my baby?" She was so great. She arranged for my husband and me to have a private tour of the maternity wing. We spent a lot of time in one of the labor and delivery rooms. That really helped me feel better. It was beautifully decorated and looked nothing like a hospital room. I sat on the bed and imagined what it would feel like giving birth in this room, and I realized I would be OK. And in class I also learned something that made a huge difference for me: I had the option of being at home for as long as possible during my labor. That made total sense to me because that's where I feel safest. My husband, on the other hand, was worried about getting me to the hospital "on time." The solution for us included knowing that, while I labored at home, we could always go to my doctor's office just to get an idea of how dilated I was. We could call in as often as we needed to touch base. In addition, we decided to hire a doula who was with me at home during labor and in the hospital. Not only was she an amazing comfort to me, her presence took the pressure off my husband. By the time I got to the hospital, I was almost six centimeters dilated. Four hours later, our son was born.

The way Jenny wound up laboring and giving birth took into account two intrinsic things about her: because of her history, she sees hospitals as scary, anxiety-provoking places and, in addition, she's someone who is highly sensitive to her environment. By being home, she was able to labor in a way that completely accommodated her particular sensitivities—feeling safe and supported in her own familiar surroundings with people she trusted. Because of this, her labor could progress in the best way possible, unobstructed by fear and anxiety. Equally as important, spending time in the hospital's maternity wing beforehand alleviated her hospital "dread factor."

Even though Jenny was resolute in her feeling that she "should" be brave, her facade couldn't help but crumble. And luckily it did *before* she went into labor because it gave her an invaluable opportunity to set herself up for a positive childbirth experience. By acknowledging her fears about hospitals and then getting the help she needed to figure out strategies for easing them, she was able to have a good, satisfying birth experience.

Making Room for the Unexpected

Preparing for birth, as much as the majority of childbirth books attest, isn't at all like planning your nursery. Crib? Check. Diapers? Check. Vaginal delivery? Maybe. The best approaches take into account that there really is no guarantee that your birth is going to go exactly the way you imagine it will. It may be that once you're actually experiencing labor, what you *thought* you'd need is different from what you actually do need while you're in it. And then there's the possibility that your *baby* may have something else in mind.

Suki: I never thought I'd be induced, but there I was—two weeks late. I had tried everything. Acupuncture, herbs, even, if you can believe it, nipple stimulation. I got to the hospital early in the morning, and my doctor started Pitocin to get things going. By early afternoon I was at one centimeter. By 7 P.M. I had inched up to three, and at midnight I was still only at three. That's when my doctor started talking about the possibility of a cesarean delivery. He said that even though my contractions were strong, the baby hadn't dropped and I wasn't dilating. He suspected that my progress was stalling for a reason but it was OK if I wanted to continue laboring for another hour or so as long as the baby and I were stable. He left the room and I lost it. I'm a dancer and in tune with my body. I just couldn't understand why this was happening to me.

> The best approaches take into account that there really is no guarantee that your birth is going to go exactly the way you imagine it will.

We all go into childbirth with preconceived notions of what we think and hope it will be like. And while visualizing a positive birth experience is a good thing, most labors and deliveries don't follow the exact script you've written in your head. Birth, by its very nature, is unpredictable. The unexpected may occur and bring with it a whole different set of circumstances than you envisioned. By being open to that, you can avoid setting yourself up to feel like a failure.

How to Leave Room for the Unexpected

- Avoid absolutes like: "I'm really athletic so labor and delivery should be a breeze for me." "Both of my sisters were two weeks early so I probably will be, too." "My mother had really fast labors and deliveries with all her babies so mine should be pretty quick." Maybe. And, then again, maybe not.

- Stay away from a detailed labor and delivery script written in ink: "My water will break while I'm sleeping (and not ruin my mattress thanks to my waterproof pad), my contractions will start up immediately, I'll go straight to the hospital (with my toes looking good having scheduled my pedicure the day before), I'll give birth to my baby, and I'll welcome visitors and open gifts shortly thereafter."

- Take loosely the description of the different stages of labor found in most pregnancy and birth books. Your contractions may hit the ground running at five minutes apart, not ten or fifteen. You might never even realize you're in "early" labor and only begin to feel like something's actually happening during "active" labor. You may have no clue that you've moved from one "stage" of labor to another. And then when you finally do reach the magical "ten," the much talked about "urge to push" may pass you right by. As much as we've been led to believe that labor and delivery follow a prescribed formula, only a few of them seem to have read that chapter word for word.

- One of the most important pieces of advice we can share with you is what we refer to as our "Leave No Stone Unturned" Theory. If your labor and delivery seem to be heading in a direction that you never expected or wanted, have someone you trust help you take a step back to review everything you've been doing so you can decide if there's anything else you might want to try or do differently. Before you even go into labor designate who this person will be— for example, your doula, partner, doctor, or midwife. That way, no matter how your birth experience winds up, you won't be left second-guessing yourself and asking, "What if?"

Suki: My doula helped me go over what we'd been doing for the last fif-teen hours—the showers, the position changes, the birth ball, and an

epidural—to try to help me dilate. And I realized that I had done every-
thing that I felt I could and wanted to do in my labor. My doula then
said something that really made sense to me. For some reason, as yet
unknown, we had to trust that despite everything I had done, this baby
had not been able to move down. Birth is a duet, not a solo. My beau-
tiful, healthy baby girl was delivered by cesarean. And they could see
what had happened—she had managed to wedge herself in my pelvis
by simply folding her little arm up over her head.

In this case, Suki had concrete evidence that, despite everything
she had been doing, her baby could not be delivered vaginally
because of her position. But sometimes you never really know why
a labor doesn't progress the way you hoped it would. And even
though you might not like what's happening, you can still end up
feeling OK about the experience if you feel supported by those
around you and are able to make decisions that are right for you
along the way.

Expectation Revelation

You come to the experience of childbirth full of expectations. The
ones that are your own and a true picture of you as well as the ones
that are your mother's, maybe some childbirth expert's, your girlfriends'. The ones that you think you should have. And the ones that
don't take into account the unpredictable nature of birth. All these
different expectations can't help but influence which options you try
on. What is key is understanding which ones aren't the right fit and
leaving them in the dressing room.

The following chapters will help you custom-fit options and
strategies to your own unique needs—emotional, psychological,
physical, spiritual—whatever it is that's important to you and makes
you who you are. Through every step of the decision-making process, from putting together your labor and delivery team to giving

birth, we'll help you cut through false expectations to get to your true ones.

Throughout this process, we can't emphasize enough the importance of talking things through. We do it with our women all the time. It's an integral part of understanding what's right for you in labor and delivery. So talk it out with a select few trusted people who really know you and can help you get to the heart of the matter without bringing up how someone else gave birth. Really take care to protect yourself from that and anything else that could cloud your decision-making process. Talk to your partner. Talk to your single girlfriend who isn't even thinking about having babies. Talk to your best friend who happens to be a guy. Talk to your doctor, midwife, childbirth instructor, or doula.

And have patience with yourself. Some choices will be more obvious than others. Some you'll know in an instant; others will dawn on you gradually. You might need to try on an entire closetful of options before you get to the ones that are right for you. And remember, you can always change your mind. If a decision you made with certainty last month starts to feel not so good this month, that's OK. You might feel discouraged, but take heart—you're really on your way to understanding what's right for you. You're just shedding those expectations and options that won't work in order to get to the ones that will.

· 3 ·

Support

This chapter is about labor support. Now, it might feel like we're getting a little bit ahead of ourselves here because you may not even be sure what you're going to want in labor and delivery, let alone what kind of support will help you get what you want. And, isn't labor support pretty much a no-brainer? Of course you're going to be supported when the time comes. Your doctor or midwife will be there. Your partner or spouse will be there. You'll have a labor nurse, right?

But what if, when the big day finally arrives, your doctor—who you trust implicitly (enough to deliver your child!)—isn't on call and another doctor in the same group, who you've met only once, is. Then there's your husband. Although he may be your best friend and comfort zone, he is so anxious he has no clue what to do during your contractions. And your labor nurse, who is very nice but a complete stranger, seems distracted. She's preoccupied with finishing up all her paperwork and anxious for her shift to be over because her child is home sick with a fever.

The thing about support is that most people don't put a heck of a lot of thought into the kind of support they're going to need during childbirth because they tend to approach it with more than a few preconceived notions: "My doctor or midwife will be with me every step of the way." "My partner will be able to anticipate and fulfill my every need." "The nurses will be angels from above" (even if you don't believe in that sort of thing, because, after all, they're delivery nurses, how could they *not* be angels?). Most people pretty much leave their support system up to chance. Many times everything turns out just fine. And then there are the times it doesn't.

Labor goes much more smoothly when you feel safe and supported, so putting together a support team that helps you feel that way is a real opportunity to set yourself up for a satisfying labor experience. Consider the following: the hormone oxytocin (which causes contractions) and endorphins (nature's "narcotic") are naturally secreted during labor. But if you are afraid or feel threatened, your body will start producing chemicals such as adrenaline that support your "fight-or-flight" response. These chemicals can actually slow down or even stop your labor. A case in point: in the wild, when a laboring animal is being hunted, labor shuts down until the animal gets to safe ground. (This brings to mind those women whose labor slows down or stops as soon as they get to the hospital.) Your mindset has a direct effect on the kinds of chemicals you'll produce in labor. That's why you need to feel safe and cared for by those around you and to trust that your needs are being met both physically and emotionally in order to labor well.

> The best kind of support happens when each person at your birth takes on the role that best suits him or her.

So let's back up a little. So far, we've been saying that when you go into childbirth with a realistic picture of who you are and what you need—whether that means getting that epidural the minute (make that the second) you get to the hospital or floating through labor in a tub listening to the strains of Native American flute music (or something in between the two)—you've set yourself up for a good birth experience. That's a major part of it. But, as you can see, the other part that's *just* as important is your support system.

At some point you're going to have to put everything you hope your childbirth experience will be into the hands of those you've chosen to be with you, whoever they are—doctor, midwife, spouse, partner, mother, sister, friend, or professional labor coach (doula). After it's all said and done, your best chance for your labor to go well and for you to feel good about your birth experience—even if things don't go the way you imagine—directly depends on the kind of support you get from this group of people.

The best kind of support happens when each person at your birth takes on the role that best suits him or her. Because really, the best support a person can give is the kind they naturally give. The doctor who's never been a hand-holder isn't going to miraculously transform into one, even though that's what you might want. And the spouse or partner who "can't look" when it comes to anything medical may not be able to get as up close and personal as you'd like.

These realizations might bring up some painful emotions. You might feel disappointed, resentful, or abandoned at a time when you're feeling pretty vulnerable. But it's extremely likely that your existing support system will be able to fill *some* of the roles that are just as important, such as "trusted doctor" and "loving partner." You might even find that you're able to adjust your expectations when it comes to what they *can't* give. And, you can always add other people to your support system who can provide what you decide you can't do without.

The Support That's Right for You

Before we help you take a look at the kind of support you might need in labor and delivery, we'd like to make something very clear. It is not about creating some "dream team" that's going to magically meet your every need and guarantee you a fairy-tale experience. There's just no such thing. It's simply about having people by your side who you feel good about and who can support you in ways that are right for you, however your birth goes.

You can put as much or as little thought into your support system as *you* want. There's no right or wrong way to do it. Remember, there are some things that you're just not going to know until you are actually experiencing labor and delivery. Even if you've had a baby before, every delivery is different. Maybe you'll find that you really don't want all that space you'd thought you'd need from your spouse or partner. Actually, you can't bear it if he leaves your side even to go to the bathroom. Or, maybe while you thought your doula would be helping you with relaxation strategies, she's now helping you get over feeling that you somehow "failed" because you want pain medication.

Keeping all this in mind, and giving yourself room to readjust your vision as you learn more about yourself and your needs, here is one way to take a realistic look at your support system. During the months and weeks leading up to your due date, as you're figuring out what kind of childbirth experience is right for you, take a look at how your doctor or midwife and spouse or partner (and whoever else you're thinking about having with you) will be able to support you in the birth picture that you envision. Mentally plug them into the experience. Given what you hope for at this moment in time, do you feel secure that they'll be there for you in the ways that you'll need them? Will they, for example, be able to help you make it through without pain medication? Or, if you begin to feel you need pain medication and that wasn't part of your original plan, can they help you come to terms with that? If avoiding a cesarean is a biggie for you, do you trust that they will do everything possible to help you not have one? Or, if you're scheduling one, will they be mindful that you'd like it to be an intimate and supportive experience? If you find yourself questioning whether or not they'll be able to "deliver," talk to them about that.

By doing this, you might find that the support people you already have are just right. Or, you might begin to see that they'll be great at some of it, but maybe not all of it. If so, this will lead you to start thinking about anyone else you might like to add to provide the rest of the support you need.

By clarifying all of this beforehand, you'll go into labor and delivery feeling comfortable that the people you've chosen to surround yourself with understand you and what you see for yourself in labor. They will work together to support you in the ways that you need to be supported, no matter how your labor and delivery unfolds. They will take care of all the details, big and small, so all you have to focus on is having your baby.

You won't have to coordinate everyone's every move (although the control freak in you may still try). You won't have to worry about your spouse or partner losing it, because if that does happen, you've arranged for someone else to be there to take care of you *and* to take care of your spouse or partner. You won't have to worry that procedures will be "done" without you understanding why and feeling OK about it. Instead of feeling isolated or alone, you will have with you a group of people you trust and can lean on. And that's at the very heart of a good birth experience.

Assembling Your Support System

Whether you've done it intentionally or not, you've already started to assemble your support system. You probably have a doctor or midwife. Maybe you interviewed quite a few to find just the right one. Perhaps your choices were limited because of your insurance plan. Or maybe you've been going to this person since you were a teenager. It really doesn't matter how this person came to be your care provider. What does matter is that you like and trust him or her and that he or she is on board with what you presently or eventually decide you'd like in childbirth. If you're in a group practice, the same goes for all of the practitioners in that practice. Depending on who's on call when you go into labor, any one of them may show up for your birth.

> What matters is that you like and trust your care provider and that he or she is on board with what you decide you'd like in childbirth.

Obviously your spouse or partner plays an important role in all of this. After all, it's the birth of his baby, too. As far as support goes, there's probably nobody else who knows you better or can provide the same sense of security or familiarity, either simply because of his presence or by taking a more active role. To what degree depends on your own needs *and* your spouse's or partner's natural abilities. In addition, you may be planning on having a close friend or family member with you or maybe even professional labor support. If you don't have a spouse or partner, that's probably even more likely.

Realistic Expectations of Your Support System

Just as the process of figuring out what you want in childbirth is an evolving one, so is figuring out what you'll need from your support givers and what they can realistically give. It could take some time to get to know your doctor or midwife and the way he or she practices. As your prenatal visits become more frequent, hopefully, you'll get that opportunity. Childbirth classes are another place where you can get a better understanding of the people you'll want with you during your delivery.

Reading through the following list of potential labor and delivery team members and what you can realistically expect from each of them can also help. It's a good way to see if the expectations you have for each of *your* team members, as they stand now, are accurate and also to see if the kind of support you need is truly the kind of support they're capable of giving. If you haven't yet signed on with a doctor or midwife, this list can help you clarify the type of practitioner who's a good match for you. It might even generate some additions to your support system that maybe you hadn't even realized were an option.

Possible Labor and Delivery Team Members

Here's what you can realistically expect from each of the possible members of your team.

Physician

First and foremost, your physician is your medical expert. He or she is there to make sure labor and delivery is going well for both you and your baby and to recognize and handle any problems that may come up.

It's important to point out that your physician's role is to oversee your labor, with *oversee* being the operative word here. Any fantasies about physicians laboring with their patients, providing minute-by-minute reassurance are probably left over from some really old-time TV shows. The reality is, if your labor is progressing smoothly, you may not see your physician continuously until you are close to delivery.

So how come this person who was so attentive during your prenatal visits now seems to be missing in action? Actually, your physician is keeping close tabs on you through your labor and delivery nurse and in the meantime is probably seeing office patients, taking care of other patients who are in labor, doing rounds, and, if it's nighttime, catching up on sleep in anticipation of seeing all those patients the next day.

While that's the standard description of what a physician does, personalities and practice styles are anything but standard. Some physicians are very interactive and include their patients in the decision-making process, giving them all their options and walking them through their choices. For example, maybe your water has broken and you've checked into the hospital but you don't have any contractions. The "interactive" physician would probably say, "You can either wait a few hours to see if contractions begin on their own and, if not, we can start you on Pitocin (the drug used to induce labor). Or we can start Pitocin now." Then he or she would guide you through the pros and cons of each choice.

The other side of the coin is the "directive" physician. Given the same scenario, he or she would probably say, "Your membranes have ruptured. We're going to start you on Pitocin to get your labor going." And that would be the end of the story unless you asked what your alternatives might be. Of course, there are many personality and practice styles between these two extremes.

You can learn a lot about the way your physician practices from the way he or she talks to you about different things during your prenatal visits. For example, when it comes to prenatal testing, does your physician explain the different tests and help you make decisions based on your feelings about testing and what you would do given the results? Or are the tests presented as strong recommendations or standard procedures? This early glimpse into the way a physician handles these issues during pregnancy is pretty much an accurate reflection of the way he or she will handle issues during labor and delivery.

We'd like to point out that there's no one way of practicing that's "better" or "more correct" than another. The way different physicians practice is the result of a combination of many things—their training, their personalities, their own personal likes and dislikes, and the kinds of experiences they've had with certain procedures or situations. All that really matters here is that your physician's practice style works for you.

In order to shed some light on just how your physician practices and if he or she is a good match for you, take a look at how you answer the following questions. If you're at a point where you're looking for a physician, some of these questions can certainly help guide you in your search.

- No matter how your physician practices, whether he or she leans toward using one particular approach or the full range of acceptable options, does he or she respect how *you'd* like to approach labor and delivery?
- If your physician's views are different from your own, for example, he or she induces anyone who goes past forty weeks, are you OK with this?
- Are you someone who needs lots of hand-holding from your doctor and likes to be walked through all your options before you're comfortable making a decision?
- Are you someone who likes your doctor to take charge and decide the best course of action for you?
- Do you care whether your physician is male or female?

Only *you* can distinguish what makes a physician better for *you*. It's to your benefit that your personality, decision-making style, and views about labor and delivery match up with your physician's. That's not to say they have to be completely aligned. Most people tend to adjust their expectations when it comes to their physicians. It doesn't have to be perfect as long as the relationship works. But if you're complete opposites, that's definitely worth taking a look at and considering a change. We think a good doctor-patient relationship includes this: your physician is able to meet you at a place where he or she feels both you and your baby's safety are not being compromised *and* you trust that you are being listened to and your concerns are being addressed.

The reality of it is, when it comes down to choosing the right practitioner for you, your choices may very well be limited by your insurance plan. Or, maybe you're in a position where you really like three out of the five doctors or midwives in your group practice and even though you're not crazy about the other two, the ones you do like are enough to keep you there. If your choices are limited and switching insurance plans is not an option or there is a chance that you might be disappointed with the practitioner who winds up being on call for your delivery, make sure in advance that the other members of your support team can supply the missing ingredients that are important to you and, if need be, act as the go-between between you and your practitioner.

Midwife

A certified nurse midwife is a registered nurse with advanced training in obstetrics and gynecology. She's trained to give routine gynecological and prenatal care and attends normal, uncomplicated labors and deliveries in hospitals and birthing centers. She can also attend home births in states where she's licensed to do so, as can certified midwives (who have a degree in midwifery but not nursing) and lay midwives (who have learned midwifery from other midwives and are not certified). Traditionally, certified nurse midwives are covered by insurance.

Similar to a physician, a midwife is there to make sure your labor and delivery are progressing safely for you and your baby. If anything

■ **How to Find a Midwife**

- Ask friends who've had babies.
- Contact birth centers.
- Research obstetrical practices that have midwives on staff.
- Check out hospital websites or call their referral line to see if there are midwives on staff.
- Contact national certifying organizations such as the American College of Nurse-Midwives (ACNM), Midwives Alliance of North America (MANA), and North American Registry of Midwives (NARM).

deviates from that, she will consult with or call in the obstetrician who backs her up. Because midwifery is based on a philosophy of one-on-one care, in theory she'll be with you throughout your entire labor and delivery, offering hands-on support to help with pain and keep your labor progressing.

The midwifery model of one-on-one care begins during pregnancy. The premise is that a midwife will spend lots of time with you during prenatal visits, helping you understand all the physical and emotional changes you're experiencing and how your baby is developing, teaching you about the importance of good nutrition and health habits, and talking with you about and helping you clarify your hopes for your labor and delivery. Historically, the midwife's approach is to let childbirth take its course with little or no intervention—including medication. But if you want medication as an option, make sure your midwife will support your choice.

Just like physicians, midwives' personalities and practice styles vary. Only you can decide if your needs are being met and the chemistry is right. Some midwives are very hands-on, seeing the patient as her own best expert and a participant in her care. Some midwives are more clinical and reserved, having less give-and-take when it comes to their patients' input. Some midwives are dogmatic about promoting "natural" birth. Others are flexible, supporting whatever it is a woman wants, including medication. Many midwives work in a group where they're just as busy as their physician counterparts, leaving little time for one-on-one care, even at deliveries. A midwife who works within a group of physicians may rotate being on call with them and, therefore, may not be the person who shows up at your birth.

Here are some questions to ask yourself to figure out whether your midwife matches up. If you're considering hiring a midwife, your answers will help you see whether that's the right choice for you.

- What's important to you about the midwifery approach to childbirth? For example, are you looking for more involvement and collaboration in your care than you believe you could get from a doctor? Can you get this/are you getting this from your midwife?
- No matter how your midwife practices, or what her philosophy is, does she respect how *you'd* like to approach labor and delivery?
- What are your feelings about pain medication and interventions? Is your midwife flexible and supportive of your goals even if they include the possibility of both?
- If your midwife's views are different from your own, for example, she encourages coping strategies like massage and laboring in a birthing pool and views medication as a last resort, are you OK with that?
- Will the midwife who does your prenatal care be the one who attends your birth?

■ Group Practice or Single Practitioner?

Whether you're with a physician or midwife, another factor that plays into the mix has to do with what kind of practice he or she is in, what comes with that particular territory, and if it *does* or *doesn't* fit your needs.

- **Single practitioners** usually attend their own births unless they're on vacation or out sick. And if that's the case, their backup will show up at your birth. If you'd find it unsettling to have a complete stranger show up to deliver your baby, consider meeting that person in advance in order to make sure you're comfortable with him or her.
- **Group practitioners** generally rotate which member is on call for deliveries. During the course of your prenatal visits, you'll typically see all the doctors or midwives in the group so you'll get a taste for each one's personality and practice style. What's key is that all of them are supportive of how you hope to approach labor and delivery. If they're not, evaluate whether or not you will have the experience you're looking for with the circumstances as they are. See if your support team can give you what they can't, or take a look at the option of switching practices.

Spouse or Partner

We think there's a lot of pressure put on a spouse or partner when it comes to childbirth. He is expected to be a coach—cheering you on, feeding you ice chips, and suggesting position changes to keep your labor progressing. He is expected to be a medical expert—knowing by the end of approximately six weeks of childbirth classes what it takes a physician eight years to learn. And he is expected to be a medical advocate—asking the right questions of the hospital staff and making clinical decisions with and for you. At the same time, he's watching you go through the most intense experience of your life, while feeling a range of emotions from helpful to helpless, and (lest we forget) having his *own* experience around the birth of his child. That's a pretty tall order for one human being to fill.

Your partner's or spouse's role in childbirth is to support you just the way he or she does in your everyday lives together, whatever that looks like. That might mean making you laugh or feel protected, staying close or maybe not so close. Nothing can take the place of the connection you have with each other and what that provides for you.

Just as you shouldn't have to turn into someone you're not to have a baby, your spouse or partner shouldn't have to either. The best kind of support that person can give you is the kind he or she feels most confident and comfortable giving. You can always look to a friend, family member, or doula to provide the rest.

Ask yourself the following questions to get a handle on how your spouse or partner can realistically support you in childbirth.

- When you're stressed out or in pain, what does your spouse or partner do for you that helps? For example, does his sense of humor help lighten things up for you? Is he right by your side, holding your hand and talking to you? Or, do you like him nearby, without any talking or touching? Whatever naturally works for the two of you in your everyday life together is what will work for you in labor and delivery.
- Are you concerned that you're going to need more or different support than your spouse or partner can naturally give? For example, you'd like to try to labor without any drugs but want that epidural standing by just in case. But you're worried that both you and your partner or spouse are going to forget all those different pain relief strategies you learned in

childbirth class. And, how can you make sure you get that epidural if you want it?

- Are you concerned that your spouse or partner, who can't even watch hospital shows on TV, isn't going to be able to handle the medical stuff? (A few words of reassurance and guidance: contrary to public opinion, we have yet to see anyone completely lose it in the birthing room. Let your spouse or partner decide how much he or she can handle and how close-up or far away he or she needs to be.)
- Are you worried that you'll feel the need to take care of your spouse of partner at a time when *you* will need to be taken care of?

Your partner's or spouse's role in childbirth is to support you just the way he or she does in your everyday lives together, whatever that looks like.

Labor Nurse

Meet your labor nurse. Unless she taught your childbirth class, led your hospital tour, or met you if you've been on the Labor & Delivery floor for care or monitoring during your pregnancy, she's a complete stranger to you. But, depending on the other people you have with you and how busy it is on the labor and delivery floor, she may very well be your lifeline. She, in theory, assumes every role that your physician and whoever else is with you doesn't. She's the connection between you and your doctor, and she just could be your labor coach on the spot.

The reality is, when it comes to labor nurses and what the nurse is like, who you get is really luck of the draw. Most of the time it all works out just fine. But sometimes it might not. Does she feel too gruff, barking orders at you? Does she seem rushed? Not warm and fuzzy enough? Too warm and fuzzy? Having some emotional connection with your nurse will help you feel safe and supported. If that's not what you're feeling, work with the nurse in charge to replace her with someone else so that you do. Yes, you heard it here first. As revolutionary as it sounds, even in this day and age of understaffed hospitals, the bottom line is, you don't have to be uncomfortable with your labor nurse. If there's no one else on your support team who can buffer you from her or provide whatever it is she can't, the nurse in charge can reassign her to a different patient and reassign another nurse to you. She'll probably feel better, too. It's just as trying for your nurse to take care of someone who clearly doesn't want to be taken care of by her.

Eva: I knew that I was about to have the labor nurse from hell when she first set eyes on me, my husband, doula, and best friend as we made our way into the birthing room. Her first words were, "You're all here for the birth?" I was too stunned and out of it to reply. But my husband's raised eyebrows and curt "yes" kept her quiet for at least a little while. My birth team did their best to shield me from her, but I remember being in the throes of a contraction and hearing her yap nonstop about the weather and how hard it was to raise teenagers. I desperately wanted her to shut up, but I was trying to keep up with my contractions and couldn't deal. And then, miraculously, it was quiet. She was gone. I learned later that my doula told the nurse, after hearing her say she had a bunch of paperwork to do, that we had everything under control and we'd call her at the nurse's station if we needed her. I guess she was OK with that because I also had my midwife with me. I still kind of regret not speaking up because maybe she would have left the room sooner. But I was grateful that my doula had.

Depending on the kind of person you are, asking for a hospital staff member to be replaced may come about as naturally to you as shoving bamboo spikes under your fingernails. Additionally, if you're up to your eyeballs in labor, you may not have the capacity or clarity of mind to say anything. You don't have to. That's why you have a support system. In retrospect, even though Eva didn't have it in her to tell the labor nurse directly, she could have privately made her feelings known to her husband or doula. And *they* could have worked out the situation that much sooner. Thankfully, Eva's doula was perceptive enough to see that the labor nurse had to go, and quiet was restored.

The answers to the following questions will help you figure out what kind of role you'll need your labor nurse to play.

- Are you confident that, leaving the labor nurse out of the equation, the people you will have with you can support you in the way you need to be supported?
- Are you OK with taking a chance on the labor nurse you'll be assigned, and if not, what are your labor support options?
- If your labor nurse is not working out, are you or a member of your support system comfortable asking that someone else be assigned to you?

Family Members and Friends

In many hospitals, you're permitted to have one other person with you in addition to your spouse or partner. This person's role varies depending on what you need: someone who gives you a sense of comfort and security that only that person can give, someone to take some of the pressure off your spouse or partner, someone to help you labor, someone to act as your go-between with the hospital staff, or someone with whom you'd really like to share your experience. This could mean your mother, your sister, your best friend, and so on. Here's a bit of advice. If your reaction to anyone on this list is "Are you kidding?!" take that as a clear sign and eliminate accordingly. We can't stress enough that the focus here is on what *you* need. If there's any chance that you'll wind up feeling like you have to take care of *them*, they're not a good choice. Let us remind you, this is about you. You're the one having the baby.

Sometimes there are good reasons *not* to have a particular person at your birth:

- You really don't want your best friend there, but she's hinted that she'd like to be and you're afraid you'll hurt her feelings if you don't invite her. We'd just like to point out that this is not a dinner party. This is the birth of your baby. You can always make her feel special by telling her you'd love it if she was one of your first visitors.
- You want your sister to be with you, but she really gets on your husband's nerves. This is the birth of *his* baby, too. Consider what having your sister there would be like for him. So cross her off your list and, again, tell her you'd love it if she was one of your first visitors.
- Your mother wants to be there with you but that's *completely* out of the question as far as you're concerned. You could tell her that it really wouldn't be fair to your spouse's mother. And did we mention you could always say you'd love it if she was one of your first visitors?

Doula

OK, we think it's a strange word, too. Even though one of us *is* a doula, she still can't get used to calling herself that. But remember what we told you about most physicians not actually laboring with you and having whoever happens to be on call show up at your delivery? Remember what we said about it being just plain luck of the draw when it comes to who will be your labor nurse? Here's where the doula finds her niche. While a doctor's or midwife's primary responsibility is the medical well-being of both mom and baby, the addition of a doula brings continuous emotional and hands-on labor support throughout the entire labor and delivery. Studies show that this kind of support significantly shortens the length of labor and reduces the need for pain medication, medical interventions, and cesarean deliveries.

A *labor doula* is childbirth lingo for a person who gives continuous support throughout labor and delivery. While some doulas have gone through certification programs, others have not. Whether or not she's certified, in order to be a seamless member of your labor support team, a doula needs to have a firm understanding of what's going on clinically as well as enough experience working with doctors, midwives, and hospital staff.

A doula's support can begin before you even get to the hospital. She helps you figure out if you're in labor, helps you find ways to labor comfortably and effectively at home in early labor, and can help you decide when it's time to go to the hospital. Once you get there, she's with you all the way through your labor and delivery, providing many things: constant reassurance, strategies for both pain relief and keeping your labor progressing, keeping you and your partner aware of where you are in the process, and acting as a sounding board when it comes to making choices. Generally, most hospitals will allow two people at your birth. If your spouse or partner is one of them, your doula fills the other slot. Insurance companies do not as of yet cover doula services, although doula services can qualify under Flexible Spending Accounts. Check to see whether your employer offers this tax-free program for medical expenses.

Ask yourself these questions to figure out if having a doula at your birth is right for you and/or whether the doula you've selected matches up:

- Is it important for you to know that you'll have one familiar person with you throughout labor and delivery?
- If your doula is part of a group or works with back-up, are you comfortable with them?
- Are you concerned that the doctor you like won't be on call or you'll wind up with a not-so-great labor nurse?
- Are you worried that your spouse or partner might not know what to do for you? Or, do you want your spouse or partner to do what he or she is comfortable doing and have somebody else take care of the rest?
- Are you hoping to avoid pain medication by relying on different comfort strategies? Or, do you want to make sure you get medication when you need it and have help figuring out what's right?

If you do decide to hire a doula, it's imperative that she feel right for *both* you and your spouse or partner. It is also important that she see herself as part of a team, working together with you, your spouse/partner, and the hospital staff instead of promoting her own

▪ How to Find a Doula
- Ask friends who've had babies.
- Ask your doctor or midwife, who may have a list of doulas that they have worked with.
- Contact Labor & Delivery at your hospital for referrals.
- See if your hospital or birth center has doulas on call (you pay a set fee, which is generally less expensive than hiring an independent doula, and you get whichever doula is on call at the time you come in).
- Check with national certifying organizations such as Doulas of North America (DONA) or Association of Labor Assistants & Childbirth Educators (ALACE) for doulas in your area.

personal childbirth agenda. Her main role is to help you accomplish whatever it is that you want for yourself.

Does Your Support System Make the Grade?

Now that you have an understanding of what you can realistically expect from all the possible players in childbirth, you can start to take a look at the members of your support system as they stand now, given their personalities, their practice styles, and the connections you have with them. As you do this, you'll begin to see what they bring to the table. Maybe it will become clear to you that you're OK with all the doctors in your group except for the one who's got the bedside manner of a latke (translation: potato pancake). Maybe you know that your spouse or partner will be with you every step of the way, but as far as helping you with labor strategies—that's just not going to happen. Perhaps you've come to see that you're going to need the kind of comfort that only your mother or sister can give. Then there's the possibility that you can't even entertain the thought of having either or them anywhere near you when you give birth.

You can take yourself through this process at whatever point you're ready, however many times you need to and whichever way you need to—in your head, in writing, or by talking it through. However you do it, you're bound to wind up with a support system that better understands how you'd like to labor and deliver and with whom you feel a connection, which therefore can best support you through it.

■ **Step-by-Step Support**

1. Take a look at each person who will be at your birth and check off what you can *realistically* expect from each of them.
2. Does the kind of support they can give match up with what you need?

3. Do you have support gaps that need filling? Consider anyone else you can add to your team.

Physician

❏ Oversees your labor—not with you continuously until you're close to delivery
❏ Interactive—includes you in decisions
❏ Directive—calls the shots
❏ Respects how you'd like to give birth
❏ Will deliver your baby
❏ May not deliver your baby

Midwife

❏ With you for entire labor and delivery
❏ May not be with you continuously for labor and delivery
❏ Respects how you'd like to give birth (including use of pain medication)
❏ Follows approach she feels is best
❏ Will deliver your baby
❏ May not deliver your baby

Spouse/Partner

❏ Can give you all the different kinds of support you need
❏ Need more or different support than spouse/partner can naturally give

Labor Nurse

❏ Who you get is luck of the draw, and you're OK with that
❏ Who you get is luck of the draw, and you're not OK with that

Doula

❏ One familiar person with you for entire labor
❏ Helps with different comfort and labor strategies to avoid pain medication

❏ Helps you figure out what kind of pain medication is right for you and helps you get it. Takes pressure off spouse/partner

❏ Works well as part of your team

❏ Respects the way you want to give birth; doesn't promote her own agenda

---

The Truth About Birth Plans

By now you should be pretty clear on the two main ingredients that make up the birth that's right for you: realistic expectations of what you would like and need in labor and delivery, and a support system that can not only help you get those needs met but also help you feel comfortable and safe so you can labor effectively. But if you're the least bit tempted, even after everything you've been reading here, to write your ticket to the kind of birth you hope for in the form of a birth plan, you might want to put that pen down.

Here's the plain and simple truth about birth plans: they just don't work. The typical birth plans of today are modeled after those that became popular in the 1980s. They were a rigid list of dos and don'ts that women wrote up in an attempt to control every aspect of their childbirth experiences, assuming the worst would be done to them if they didn't. Variations of these birth plans can even be downloaded right off the Internet, complete with bulleted lists of every imaginable childbirth procedure and preference. With the click of a mouse you can put a check in whichever little box you choose to create and print out your "dream" birth. It's all there and then some, whether you want pain medication or not (and if so, *exactly* what kind), how you want your baby to be monitored during labor (fetoscope, Doppler, external or internal fetal monitor), and so on—right down to what's OK to give your baby in the newborn nursery (i.e., ixnay on the sugar water, OKway on the pacifier).

We'd like to offer two pieces of wisdom. One, birth can't be planned (although, again, the control freak in you may try). And two, if you feel you need to safeguard against your doctor's approach with a list of procedures that you don't want, that's a clear sign you're with the wrong doctor and you seriously need to consider a change. While we can't vouch for every practitioner out there, it's probably safe to say that most don't believe, for example, that women actually *want* to be hooked up to a million monitors or have long, drawn-out labors and wind up with cesareans.

Another reason birth plans don't work is they're based on an idealistic version of childbirth, making them a sure setup for disappointment. For example, according to Lamaze, you'll be most comfortable and your baby will move down more easily if you walk or "slow dance" during labor. So you go ahead and put that into your birth plan. But what happens once you're actually in labor and you just don't have it in you? All you want to do is curl up in bed in the fetal position, but you're feeling like a failure because you're not moving around. And according to those Bradley classes you took, any kind of pain medication is unsafe for your baby. So you note that in your birth plan. But now your contractions are peaking, and those abdominal breathing exercises just aren't working. You really want something for the pain, but you feel like you'd be selling out if you took anything. There are just some things that won't be clear to you until you're actually experiencing labor for yourself. And that's why basing what you'll need on some childbirth expert's version of labor doesn't work unless it completely matches your own.

The Good Birth Wish List

Instead of a birth plan, we recommend what we call The Good Birth Wish List. What is the major difference between the two? The wish list is really not a plan at all. As head of your birth team you are sharing your expertise about you—your hopes, your fears, your likes, your dislikes, your dreams, and your aspirations for this birth. This labor wish list can include the things that you would like and/or the things that you would like to avoid, taking into account how your labor and delivery are progressing, how you're feeling at the time, and the judgment of your care providers. It can also include anything about you that you'd like to share, especially with the hospital staff you haven't yet met.

> As head of your birth team, in your Good Birth Wish List you are sharing your expertise about you—your hopes, your fears, your likes, your dislikes, your dreams, and your aspirations for this birth.

Your labor wish list can be in whatever form you're comfortable with. You can talk about your wishes during a prenatal visit, or, if there's a lot you need to share, you can continue the conversation over the course of many visits. If you're the type who thinks best "on paper," you can write it down and use it as a starting point for discussions with your doctor or midwife. It can be stored in your chart and when the time comes, your chart will be sent over to Labor & Delivery where your nurse can read it and get a sense of who you are and what's important to you.

Look at this wish list as an opportunity to share what's important *to* you and *about* you. For example, "It took me three go-arounds of in vitro to get pregnant. We'd really like to be able to bond with our baby for as long as possible after she's born." Or, "Instead of the doctor or nurse announcing the sex of our baby, my husband would like to do that." Or, "I'd really like to be able to move around during labor. Instead of an IV, I'd prefer a heparin lock" (the initial part of the IV without the tubing and bag of IV fluid). Or, "As long as the baby is doing well, I'd like to have fetal monitoring only when necessary, which I have discussed with my doctor ahead of time."

Being open about what's important to you is to your benefit, and to the benefit of your caregivers. Unless you tell them, there's really no way they can know that you might need sensitivity and extra tender loving care about specific things. For example, maybe you've experienced sexual abuse and the thought of having an unfamiliar resident check to see how dilated you are makes you extremely uncomfortable. Or, you're prone to panic attacks and you're afraid being in a hospital environment is going to bring one on. Perhaps certain procedures, such as an IV, make you skittish. Your labor wish list can be an invaluable way for your caregivers to get to know you better and address your specific needs.

Here are some examples of how you can make your wishes known:

To the Labor and Delivery Staff,

I'm due to give birth at your hospital soon and I wanted to share some things about me in advance of the big day. Although I'm hoping to make it through without pain medication, I'm not ruling it out. And, if I do wind up needing it and that entails an IV, I wanted to let you know that I've had a few bad experiences with getting my blood drawn, which have been pretty anxiety-producing. I've been told that it's challenging to find a "good" vein because my veins are small. Should I need an IV, I'd really like the nurse who's most likely to get it on the first try to do it.

With Real Appreciation,

Michelle Lewis

Dear Dr. Rivera and Hospital Staff,

I'm planning on having an epidural during labor. As we've discussed during my prenatal visits, I'm hugely relieved to know that an epidural will be available to me as soon as I feel I need it—even if I'm just a few centimeters dilated—because I'm really concerned about the pain. I understand that both the baby and I need to be stable. Please let the hospital staff know that you and I have discussed my needs so that we can do whatever is needed to facilitate my getting an epidural as soon as possible.

Thank you so much for your help in this matter.

Sincerely,

Lyn Fung

To the Doctors of Ocean Side Specialists,

As you all know, getting and staying pregnant has been a long, heart-wrenching road for both David and me. After two miscarriages and numerous fertility treatments, we still can't quite let ourselves believe that we'll soon be parents. Even though we both know that the baby's fine and she and I will have excellent care during labor and delivery, we're really anxious about the birth considering the many disappointments we've experienced to get to this point. Once I'm in labor, it would really help us to have as much explanation as possible about what's happening every step of the way and reassurance that the baby is OK. We know that your continued support will go a long way in alleviating our worries.

Thank You in Advance,

Barbara and David Kosta

Changing Your Doctor or Midwife

As we've said earlier, most people adjust their expectations when it comes to their practitioner. And certain things are just not worth switching for—especially after you've made an emotional investment in this doctor or midwife. What really matters is that you like and trust this person. But if you come to the conclusion that your birth philosophies just don't match up or the chemistry is really off, it might be time to consider making a change.

This can feel like a very big deal to you, particularly if you've been with this practitioner for a long time or it's later on in your pregnancy, because you've built a relationship with this person. The thought of switching can bring up all sorts of uncomfortable feelings, including guilt about leaving and guilt about hurting his or her feelings, and it can be anxiety-producing because you may not know the person you're ultimately going to wind up with after you leave—the opposite of feeling safe and secure.

June: Very early on in my pregnancy, we moved out of the city and into the suburbs. I liked my doctor—he came highly recommended by a close family friend and I had been with him since college—so finding someone closer to home never even dawned on me. But as I began to see more and more of him at my prenatal appointments, I slowly started to realize that his grandfatherly attitude, which was reassuring when I was in my twenties, wasn't cutting it now. I was coming in with lots and lots of questions, and his answers made it very clear that he wasn't willing to entertain the thought of anything other than the way he did things. I really wanted a birth without a lot of medical intervention and that's just not the way he practiced. Still, I felt this weird loyalty to him. He'd been my doctor for all of my adult life.

The needs you have of a practitioner at a time in your life when you're not even thinking about having a baby (and most likely doing everything possible *not* to have one!) are quite different from the needs you have when you're pregnant and getting closer to that inescapable day when you'll give birth. Think about it. You've gone from seeing your doctor for a total of maybe five minutes once a year for a Pap smear to now coming in with an endless inventory of questions that up until now you never thought to ask or even had reason to. The way your practitioner answers these questions helps you gauge how he or she practices. And sometimes you begin to see, as June did, that what worked for you before pregnancy, isn't working now. And there you are, in an uncomfortable limbo, wondering, should I stay or should I go?

> The decision to switch care providers is really a matter of weighing what's troubling you and if you can work that out versus the benefits you might get if you switched.

Pragmatically speaking, the decision whether to switch or not is really a matter of weighing what's troubling you and if you can work that out versus the benefits you might get if you switched. So look at what's troubling you. Your first move might be a conversation with your physician. Even if he or she practices in a very specific way, your physician might still be able to accommodate what you'd like in labor and delivery. Or maybe you can reach a comfortable medium. You can also ask yourself if adding someone else to your birth team would make a difference, allowing you to adjust your expectations. In addition, it may also be helpful to interview one or two people you think might be a better choice to see whether you'd feel like you were trading up for what's important to you. This way, whether you stay in the practice you're in or you move on, you'll be less likely to undermine your decision by asking yourself at the end of your birth experience—what would have happened *if*?

This whole process can leave you feeling pretty anxious. It might help to know that the anticipation of switching is *much* more anxiety-producing than the switch itself. Once you've acknowledged that something's not right and you make the move to someone who is better for you, you're operating from a place of strength and knowing rather than resignation or mistrust. And the relief you feel makes it totally worth it.

> *June: On top of everything I was feeling about my doctor, as I got bigger and bigger, I started thinking about being in labor and having to endure that long car ride into the city, maybe during rush hour or a snowstorm. I had visions of my husband frantically pulling off the road and delivering the baby in the back of our car with the hazard lights flashing. I was really stressing about all of it but feeling too stuck to do anything. During a chance conversation with my neighbor I found out that for her second baby she switched from a city practice to a great local doctor whose office was a few towns away. I bit the bullet and made an appointment. And I wound up feeling really comfortable there. The clincher for me was that this new doctor actually trained under my city doctor and had a lot of respect for him. I wrote a letter to my old doctor thanking him for his care over the years and explained my need to be closer to home. Writing to him made me feel better. I signed on with my new doctor and that was that.*

Once you've decided to make the switch, all you have to do is call your practitioner's office and have them fax or mail you the forms you need to fill out so your records can be sent to your new practitioner. Your exit can be as simple as that. If you're asked why, you can say as much or as little as you feel comfortable saying. It's much easier when your switch has to do with insurance coverage or, as in June's case, if you want to deliver closer to home.

But if it's more about the practitioner, you may feel the need to address the personal piece and get some closure. You can do that through a conversation in the office, by phone, or in a letter. Whichever way you do it, it's not your responsibility to take care of your practitioner. All you need to do is take care of you. It's a win-win situation all around. You need to feel good about the care you're getting, and any doctor is going to feel better being with a patient that's happy with the care he or she is providing. Remember, it's never too late to make a change. You can do that right up to your actual labor and delivery.

Putting together a good support system can be a lot like match-making. Everybody's support profile will be different based on their own unique hopes and needs. Yours might be: hands-on midwife, reassuring husband, birth-ball-toting doula. Whereas, the support profile of the woman giving birth one room away might be: take-charge doctor, anesthesiologist at the ready, partner standing by (but not too close by), and mother in the visitor's waiting room under lock and key. But, unlike *romantic* matchmaking, instead of relying on one person to be your be-all and end-all, you put yourself in the capable hands of a group of people—your doctor or midwife, your spouse or partner, your labor nurse, a good friend or family member, a doula—you know and trust will support you in the very ways you need to be supported.

· 4 ·

Hospital, Birth Center, or Home Birth?

Where Will *You* Be When You Pass Go?

In most cases, where you have your baby has to do with wherever your doctor or midwife has admitting privileges. But the opposite could hold true. You might choose your birth location first, practitioner second. Maybe you're drawn to a particular hospital because it's associated with a prestigious medical school or has a crackerjack neonatal intensive care unit. Or maybe it's because you'll be assured a private room (and the offer of a champagne dinner on your last night doesn't hurt either!). You may be attracted to a particular birth center because of its homey atmosphere, its reputation for family-centered maternity care, and its Jacuzzi. Perhaps you feel the only way you're going to have the birth that's right for you is at home sweet home.

Your personal preferences and a pinch (or a whole handful) of reality all play into where you end up having your baby. You may find your choices are pretty limited because of your insurance plan. Or, existing health issues, pregnancy complications such as high blood pressure, or obstetrical issues such as a breech baby may mean your only option is a hospital birth with a doctor. Your decision on where you have your baby will come from a balance of what you can and can't live without, your insurance coverage, and possibly considerations that have to do with your well-being and your baby's.

The following sections will help you clarify the best place for you to have your baby.

Hospital Birth

Do you want to give birth with a doctor or midwife and have the full gamut of medical expertise and pain medication available at a moment's notice?
A hospital provides the reassurance of immediate medical capability while accommodating a range of childbirth preferences—from whether you want an epidural early on (*you'd* really like to know if they can start it in your ninth month) to a "wait-and-see" stance to a medication-free birth. What's key here is making sure that you and your practitioner are on the same page. For example, you've discussed in advance of labor that you'd rather not have an IV started unless you really need one, or you prefer intermittent instead of continuous fetal monitoring so you can move around. In addition to your spouse or partner, you'll most likely be able to have another person with you if you want.

Although we can't vouch for every hospital, many have responded to the consumer-driven preference for low-tech, less hospital-like birthing rooms. Some look more like hotel rooms, others like homey birth center rooms with showers and sometimes tubs. Many come fully loaded with a rocking chair and a recliner (which can double as a sleeper for your spouse or partner). Bring your birth ball and whatever other labor-coping tools you need. Your length of stay is primarily driven by your insurance coverage, but generally it is forty-eight hours for a vaginal birth and three to four days for a cesarean delivery. The clock starts ticking the moment your baby is out of your body (i.e., if you deliver at 11 P.M., you have only one hour left of what now counts as your first day, but if you deliver at 1 A.M., your first day has twenty-three hours left to go).

Tina: I unexpectedly got pregnant shortly after my husband and I moved to another state. I didn't have a doctor because we were new to the area and when I started asking around I kept hearing that whoever I went with, I should definitely deliver at the new hospital a few towns away. The labor and delivery rooms were supposed to be gorgeous—bright and airy—and the hospital was really up on advances in epidural anesthesia, even though I wasn't thinking I was headed in that direction. The community hospital closest to my house paled in comparison. It looked pretty old and dingy from the outside and the labor and delivery rooms didn't get good reviews at all. I decided to schedule a tour of the new hospital and was immediately sold. The maternity floor was phenomenal, and the nurse who showed me around was so nice. She gave me names of doctors who deliver there, and I wound up finding a group that I'm really comfortable with. As far as getting an epidural, I'm waiting to see how I feel once I'm in labor, but it's reassuring to know it's available if I need it and that I'll be having my baby in such a beautiful, welcoming place.

Hospital Savvy

Depending on what's important to you, here are some questions you might ask when considering whether a particular hospital is the right one for you:

- Are there neonatologists on staff just in case (pediatricians who specialize in premature and newborn infants)?
- What is your neonatal intensive-care capability if I deliver early?
- What kinds of high-risk situations would require me or my baby to be transferred to another hospital?
- Will residents take care of me as well as my doctor will?
- Is the hospital staff supportive of low-intervention birth (such as intermittent monitoring and no routine IVs)?

- Is a walking epidural an option? (See Chapter 9 for more on walking epidurals.)
- Are midwives on staff?
- Can I have a doula? If I need a cesarean delivery, can my doula go into surgery with me?
- How many people can be with me during labor?
- Do the labor and delivery rooms have showers, tubs, or Jacuzzis?
- Is the hospital supportive of family-centered maternity care (rooming in, breast feeding, and partners staying the night)?
- How many private postpartum rooms are there and how often are patients doubled up?

Birth Center Birth

Do you want to give birth with a midwife in a nonhospital environment without an epidural and interventions, such as Pitocin, to help labor progress? Do you want the security of being located next to or actually in a hospital?

At a birth center you'll typically receive prenatal care from its staff of midwives and when the time comes, you'll labor and have your baby in a birthing room that looks very much like a bedroom. The medical stuff is hidden behind Laura Ashley or Pottery Barn–like décor. In addition to your spouse or partner (and doula if you've hired one), you can have as many family members or friends with you as you'd like. The focus here is lots of hands-on support during labor along with epidural and intervention-free births, although either one is a short walk, car ride, or ambulance ride away. If you're at a free-standing birth center, you need to be comfortable with the possibility that if anything comes up in your labor that falls outside birth center guidelines (e.g., you need Pitocin to strengthen your contractions or you develop a fever—anything other than normal changes in your baby's heart rate or your baby needs forceps or vacuum) you'll be transported to a nearby hospital with which the birth

▣ **Are You a Candidate for a Birth Center Birth?**

Certain conditions that might be preexisting or that come up during your pregnancy or even labor could "risk you out" (prevent you from being a candidate) for a birth center birth. These conditions might include heart disease, high blood pressure, diabetes, anemia, preterm labor, vaginal bleeding, twins, a previous cesarean delivery, a pregnancy that goes beyond forty-two weeks, a breech baby, abnormal fetal heart rate, and a baby that needs vacuum or forceps to be born.

center has an arrangement. A crucial component for you may be that your team comes too, including your midwife, even though you'll be under the care of your back-up physician (with whom you've probably had at least one routine prenatal visit).

Some hospitals actually have birth centers in-house where doctors as well as midwives deliver babies. The benefit of an in-hospital birth center is that you won't have to go far (maybe to a different floor or just down the hall) if you need medical support or want an epidural. But unlike their free-standing counterparts, they might not completely adhere to the "nonintervention" philosophy of giving birth. Make sure they offer what you're looking for *before* you sign on. In order to be covered by your insurance, free-standing birth centers need to be accredited and licensed by the state and have licensed care providers. You generally go home within twelve to twenty-four hours after you've given birth.

Marci: I had my first baby at a birth center and it was a wonderfully calm, laid-back experience. I was monitored only every so often and I felt completely free to labor however I needed to. In the beginning I wandered around a bit and then as my contractions got stronger I wound up in and out of the Jacuzzi. There was a kitchen down the hall, which was perfect because my husband, after not eating a thing all day because he was so charged up, ended up getting ravenous. I even ate a bit of applesauce.

When it came time, I pushed, sometimes squatting, sometimes sitting on a birth stool, but ultimately was most comfortable in bed. Our son Sawyer was born after two and half hours of pushing, and I didn't even tear. My husband and I were just ecstatic over the way the birth went, so when I got pregnant with baby number two, there was no doubt in our minds that she would be born at the birth center. My second labor was so different from my first. It just piddled along. So when my midwife suggested rupturing my membranes to try to get it moving, I was in full agreement. But then my baby's heart rate began to drop with each contraction and my midwife said, very calmly, that she felt it would be best to go over to the hospital for closer monitoring. So there I was, stark naked and sweating from labor, with my husband and my doula helping me into my sweatpants. They walked me, one under each arm, across the parking lot and up the driveway to the hospital. I tried to get settled in my hospital room, but I was pretty unnerved by the move and the hospital room felt sterile and foreign. Intuitively, my doula shut the door and dimmed the lights to re-create the serene ambiance of my birth center room. And she reassured me that, even though this birth wasn't happening the way I thought it would, I was completely safe and very close to meeting my baby girl. Miranda was born barely an hour later. Although she had needed closer monitoring, she was perfectly healthy in every way. Looking back at my births, I feel like I've experienced the best of both worlds. The cozy, relaxed atmosphere of the birth center along with the reassurance of modern medicine.

Birth Center Savvy

Depending on what's important to you, here are some questions you might ask when considering whether a particular birth center is the right one for you:

- Is the birth center accredited by the Commission for the Accreditation of Birth Centers?

- What are the guidelines for giving birth here?
- Is pain-relief medication such as Demerol an option?
- For what reasons might I need to be transported to a hospital?
- How will I get to the hospital?
- If I'm transported to a hospital, will my back-up physician take over along with my midwife?
- Will those with me be allowed to stay with me at the hospital?

■ Taking the Water Birth Plunge

The concept of laboring in a birthing pool was introduced in France in the 1970s by French obstetrician Michel Odent. Immersion in warm water (97°F, which is about body temperature) was found to reduce the need for pain medication and speed up labor. Odent stresses that a woman should never feel like a prisoner in the pool. You might want to go in and out. And you might want to give birth *outside* of the pool. Listening to your body will tell you what's right for you.

Here's what a water birth looks like. You're immersed in a birthing pool up to your breasts. The goal is to completely cover your belly because the feeling of weightlessness takes the pressure off your abdomen. You can move around and get into whatever positions you find comfortable. Your spouse or partner can even be in the pool with you. When you're ready, you push your baby out into the water and he or she is gently brought up to the surface. Babies instinctively wait until they get above water to take their first breath.

Some call the pain relief you get from giving birth in water "an aquadural." If you're considering a water birth, some birth centers and a few hospitals do offer the option of delivering your baby in the water and birthing tubs can be rented for a home birth.

Home Birth

Do you want to give birth with a midwife and are deeply committed to a birth without pain medication or interventions? Do you feel that being at home is the best way to accomplish that and it's the safest and most natural place for you to have your baby?

Home births are attended by certified nurse midwives or certified midwives (who don't have nursing degrees but learn midwifery skills through apprenticeships or at independent midwifery schools). Lay midwives (midwives trained by other midwives and are not certified) also attend home births. You may choose to see an obstetrician throughout pregnancy and then have a midwife deliver your baby. Or you may choose to have a midwife handle both your prenatal care and delivery.

At the heart of the home birth philosophy is the belief and trust that the body knows how to give birth. Therefore, birth is allowed to happen in its own way and in its own time. A home birth can be as family-centered as you'd like, with those you care about at your side or nearby during your labor and birth. Or, it can be a very private, intimate experience with just you, your spouse or partner, and your midwife. You might also choose to add a doula to the home birth equation. Preparation for a home birth should include having a doctor for medical backup and putting transportation plans in place should you or your baby need hospital care.

> *Amy: I had been seeing various midwives for my gynecological care ever since I was in college, so when I got pregnant it was just a given that a midwife would deliver my baby. The group that I'm with has admitting privileges at my local hospital. But when I really started to think about it, I had a hard time envisioning myself giving birth there. I'm a big believer in alternative medicine and my husband's a chiropractor. We've both pretty much avoided the traditional medical route for our entire adult lives. When I talked to my midwife about my misgivings about*

being in a hospital environment, she reassured me that even though I'd be in one, my desire to give birth without drugs or interventions would be fully supported. But, if I thought that being in a hospital was going to make me anxious and uncomfortable, giving birth at home was also an option, as long as everything was going well with the baby and me. The idea of having my baby at home felt both scary and exciting. As my husband and I went back and forth over the possibility, it began to feel a lot more right than being in a hospital. We made the decision to have a home birth and started getting ready. We met the back-up physician who would care for me if I needed to be transported to the hospital and we did a dry run to the emergency room, which was just ten minutes away. We got a space heater so our room would be nice and toasty after the baby was born. And we found a pediatrician we really liked. Kaili was born after twelve hours of labor in the very same bed in which she was conceived. Although labor was harder than I thought it would be, I never once felt scared or that I would be better off in the hospital. It was the best decision I could have made.

Unlike Amy, most women who give birth at home are second- or third-time moms. Having a successful childbirth track record boosts their faith in the birth process and their confidence that both they and their baby will be fine. But whether it's your first baby or your fourth, the motivation for having a home birth is as individual as the women having them. Like Amy, you might feel safer outside a hospital. You also might feel having your baby at home is the best way to avoid any kind of intervention. Or, you might want to give your other children the opportunity to be included and the only way for that to happen is at home (although that *can* happen at a birth center and at some hospitals).

If that's the case, it's really important to prepare siblings who may be present at birth for that experience in advance. There are videos, DVDs, and books specifically geared toward siblings that can help them understand what's going to happen at the birth. Common wis-

---

▪ Is a Home Birth Safe?

As with pretty much everything regarding your childbirth options, you'll find research that supports home births and research that doesn't. The American College of Obstetricians and Gynecologists (ACOG), of which one of the authors of this book is a member, maintains that the safest place to give birth is in a hospital. Yet studies done in Great Britain and the Netherlands (where more than one-third of women give birth at home) show home birth to be a safe option for healthy women with low-risk pregnancies. (One of the other authors of this book has had two home births right here in the United States.) Just as with birth center births, there are preexisting conditions or conditions that can arise during your pregnancy or labor that would "risk you out" of a home birth. (See the sidebar Are You a Candidate for a Birth Center Birth?)

---

dom is to pair one adult (someone who's not part of your support team) with each sibling at the birth. That adult's sole job is to be responsible for whatever that child may need, including being able to come and go freely, which in turn leaves your support team available to you.

Home Birth Savvy

Here are some questions you might ask when considering whether a home birth is right for you:

- Is the nearest hospital less than thirty minutes away?
- Am I confident that my midwife can assess any risks that would indicate the need for me to be transported to the hospital?
- Am I confident that medical care will be expediently available if needed?

- Who will be the physician backing up my midwife and who will be responsible for my baby's medical care?
- What kind of postpartum visits does the midwife offer?
- What kind of postpartum help will I arrange for after the baby is born?
- When everything is said and done, am I confident that I won't second-guess myself about having a home birth?

When your decision is based on the things that are important to you, it can't help but be the right one.

Making the Choice

No matter where you end up having your baby, what matters most is that you've arrived at that place using your expertise about you. When your decision is based on the things that are important to you, it can't help but be the right one. So look at what you'd like and need—whether it's being at a hospital or a birth center that's close to home, being willing to go the distance for one that's not, knowing that your baby will have top-notch neonatal care if he or she needs it, or giving birth in the comfort of your own bedroom. It may be that you won't find everything you're hoping for all in one place. If so, weigh the pros and cons and make your decision based on the pieces that are most important to you, letting them be your guide. You'll land right where you need to be.

· 5 ·

Labor Signs

Now that you don't have a stitch of maternity clothing left that fits, and you've come to your senses that it would be a real waste to go out and buy more, it's probably dawning on you, consciously or subconsciously, that the countdown to labor and delivery has begun. Maybe you've settled yourself contentedly in for the long haul, savoring every last day of your pregnancy (you probably still have something left to wear). Or, maybe, you want to fast-forward to that moment when you actually get to meet this person who's been camping out inside you. Perhaps, contrary to everything you've been led to believe, pregnancy hasn't been all that blissful. It's been downright hard, and giving birth yesterday wouldn't be soon enough for you.

So you turn the last calendar page hanging between you and your due date. Your bag is packed. You've got the requisite number of Onesies and receiving blankets. You've washed them all (in baby detergent, of course) and put them away in perfect little "Baby Gap–like" piles. Or, your shower gifts are the only piles in your house (pointing skyward on the dining room table). Your baby's crib is on backorder. And you'll be packing for the hospital in between contractions. No matter how ready or not ready, how prepared or unprepared you are—logistically, materialistically, emotionally—the story of having a baby usually begins the same way for everyone: trying to figure out if you're in labor or let alone close to it.

The Waiting Game

The way you handle the last few weeks of waiting for a sign that your labor is starting will be some version of the way you naturally handle the anticipation of something big. Along with the excitement or happiness or whatever it is you're feeling as you await the birth of your baby, depending on your personality, you could be feeling other things, too.

If you're the kind of person who likes to know what's happening to you every step of the way, you might feel like you've lost your bearings and you're at the mercy of these sometimes elusive labor signs. If you like to be the one holding the reins, the lack of control you feel might drive you crazy. If you're the type who likes to keep things moving right along, you might feel stalled or in limbo. And if you like to take your time to analyze and process what's going on for you, not having any labor signs to process may leave you feeling like a mouse lost in a maze.

Every single one of these feelings is right on. You're in a holding pattern on the threshold of something monumental—giving birth to your baby. On top of that, you have no idea when you'll be crossing that threshold. It could be weeks or it could be days. Here are some things that might help ease this state of "suspended animation."

If activity makes you feel like you're moving forward, making it "baby related" might help you feel like you're accomplishing something.

- If you're doing birth announcements, think about picking them out or making them now and preaddress all those envelopes.
- If you're a shutterbug, stock up on photo albums. You're going to need a place for all those snapshots of your baby. And while you're at it, pick up a brag book that you can stash

in your purse. This way you won't come up empty-handed when someone inevitably asks, "Do you have any pictures?"

- Fill in the "family history" pages of your baby's birth book.
- Get "crafty." If knitting or crocheting is your thing, make a newborn cap or soft socks for your little one. If you embroider, decorate a bib or baby blanket. Or, if you needlepoint, make a small pillow or wall hanging for your baby's room.
- Stock the fridge and freezer. Make some meals that you can freeze so you won't have to think about making dinner every night once your baby is born.
- Take care of *you*. Get a manicure, pedicure, haircut, color, and so on. Finding time for these things can be challenging once you have a newborn.

If you need to process and/or talk about how the waiting is making you feel:

- Connect with those who can nurture you. Talk with a friend who's a good listener and can just be there for you. Or, talk to someone who's a good adviser and can help you put into perspective what you're going through.
- Chat online. Go to your favorite pregnancy and childbirth website and commiserate with women who are in your exact same position.
- Write it down. E-mail a friend, keep a journal, or write a letter to your baby telling him or her what was happening for you just before he or she was born. Kids love nothing better than to hear stories about themselves when they were babies, even when they were in utero. If you prefer to draw what you're feeling, create and illustrate a "Waiting for You" picture book. It's guaranteed to be the best-read book in your child's library.

Here Comes a Sign (You Think . . .)

Then, as you're doing what you can to alleviate the craziness of feeling like a mother hen waiting for her egg(s) to hatch, you get what you think is a sign. And that opens up an entirely different can of emotions. You might feel exhilarated and relieved—you were beginning to feel like you were gestating a baby elephant. You might feel anxious and unsure—wondering what's going to happen next and whether you can handle it. Doubts about *what* it is you're feeling could also creep in. If you're at work, you may be debating whether you should go home or not and if you should call your spouse or partner. What if it's not the real deal?

Even if you're not completely certain that labor is starting for you, but you need some support, then get it. Call your doctor for feedback. If need be, have someone stand in for your spouse or partner until you know for sure you're in labor. Give yourself the space to "not be sure" about what's going on. You've never done this before. Just like you, your spouse or partner doesn't know what's going on either. That's OK. You'll figure it out together. One contraction at a time.

> If you're not completely certain that labor is starting for you, but you need some support, then get it.

When Labor Takes You by Surprise

Labor doesn't always begin with clear-cut signs and a slow, methodical buildup. You may spend your last few weeks of pregnancy, searching for clues only to find out that your labor has slipped in under the radar screen. You might learn at one of your last few prenatal visits that—surprise, surprise—unbeknownst to you, you're walking around a few centimeters dilated. That's bound to get you either pretty excited or pretty terrified (or a combination of both!). How soon full-fledged labor will kick in is anybody's guess. It could be a matter of hours, and then again, it could be days. Or, maybe signs have been there all along, but because they're so unfamiliar it's only once you get to the other end that you're able to look back and say, "Oh, *that's* what that was."

> **Brooke:** *Sometime on Saturday I started to notice that my underwear was continuously damp. Not soaked or anything, just slightly wet. I didn't know what it was. I figured maybe it was discharge, or that the baby was really pressing on my bladder and I was leaking urine. I wasn't due for three more weeks so I really didn't pay that much attention to it. I had a prenatal appointment scheduled for Monday so I figured I'd just mention it to my doctor then. When I did casually tell her, I have to admit I was a little taken aback at how it really seemed to get her attention. She tested the fluid I was leaking and what she said next was a complete shock. My water had broken. I didn't even believe her. How could that be? I wasn't due for three weeks.*

When labor hits you by surprise, it may leave you feeling a bit ungrounded. You might need more time to process what's happening. Or, if you like to be the one calling the shots, you might feel scared and out of control. Whether labor sneaks up on you or you've been desperately waving a plucked chicken around your pregnant belly, intoning labor to begin, there's also something else happening. On some level, consciously or subconsciously, you know that what's in store for you is pretty darn big—you're giving birth *and* becoming a mother. Although your body and baby may be ready, your head may not be.

Brooke: After I got over my initial shock, I realized I had been feeling crampy all morning. My doctor said to go home, pack my bag, and make my way to the hospital because, by this time, my membranes had probably been ruptured for over forty-eight hours and she felt it was time to get my labor going. My husband came home from work right away. He was thrilled, but I have to say I wasn't. I had heard that you reach a point at the end of your pregnancy where you're so uncomfortable you can't wait to get the baby out. But I didn't feel that way at all. It all felt so surreal, too soon. I hadn't planned for this. We walked to a park near our apartment. It was a gorgeous spring day and the park was filled with little kids playing and babies in strollers. We sat on a bench and talked about how unreal it was that soon we'd be bringing our baby here. We laughed about what kind of parents we'd be and tried to guess what our baby would be like. When we got home I took a long shower and organized what we were taking to the hospital, and then we got in the car. I felt much readier for whatever was coming next. I just needed that extra time to get over the shock of it.

Once you're actually in labor, you may need some time for your head to catch up with what's going on with you physically. Because Brooke's labor began slowly, she was able to take some time for herself to get used to the idea that soon she would be giving birth. When labor and delivery happen unexpectedly, sometimes that adjustment period happens *after* the baby is born.

Every labor story opens in its own way. Some announce themselves with gusto. Others might be a little tentative and shy until they warm up. Some show up early; some show up late. And with some, you might not realize that, until you start feeling contractions, there were little signs along the way that you hadn't picked up on. Maybe you weren't really looking for them because your due date is weeks away. But here you are in labor. Go figure. And that pretty much sums up the inexact science of how labor begins. The road map is different for everyone. All you can do is read the signs as best you can. You'll get there just fine.

Putting Together the Labor Signs Puzzle

So just how will you be able to tell if you're in labor? Your attitude might be pretty laid-back—you figure you'll just know. Maybe you've been fixating on every bodily sensation from the moment you got pregnant (you swear you could even tell when that sperm made contact with that egg).

Putting together the pieces of the labor signs puzzle can be a little like searching for a needle in a haystack. Some of the signs may not be so obvious and some may pass you right by. And sometimes they're only recognizable after the fact—it may be, until there's no doubt that you *are* in labor, that you realize you've been having signs all along.

But before we go any further, we need to let you know that we are not at all responsible for what these labor signs are called. You are now about to enter labor terminology boot camp. So if you happen to be anywhere from somewhat shy to completely grossed out about bodily functions, this next section will test your mettle. It's almost downright impossible to be sensitive or discreet about some of these signs. And we're sorry to break it to you that, not only will you have to figure out if you're having them, you'll actually have to talk about them, sometimes in greater detail than you'd like, with your care providers. But there is a silver lining. The fact that you're having these signs means you're that much closer to having your baby.

Prelabor Signs

About four to six weeks before your labor even starts, you might get some clues that your pregnancy is winding down and your body is getting ready for labor. The clues can be so subtle or happen so gradually that you barely even notice them. And you shouldn't feel any pressure to have to detect them because having them doesn't mean that you're *in* labor. Stronger Braxton Hicks contractions and dropping are two signs that let you know you're getting closer.

Braxton Hicks Contractions

One indication that you're moving ahead is that your Braxton Hicks contractions, which started about your fifth month, get stronger. Why this happens is really pretty amazing. These contractions warm up and tone your uterus to get it ready for childbirth. They're actually building its strength without you even having to lift a finger. (Why can't our entire body do that?)

Braxton Hicks contractions don't hurt, but they might feel a little weird. You may notice a tightening of your belly, starting from the top and spreading down. It could feel like your baby's rolling from one side to another or that all of a sudden your belly's rock hard or bunched up like a ball. Your belly will stay that way for a bit and then go back to the way it was.

Now, even though you may not think you're having Braxton Hicks contractions, you are. And just because maybe you can't *sense* them, you aren't failing Pregnancy 101. Braxton Hicks contractions are doing their job, part of which is moving your baby down into your pelvis—sort of like NASA staging the space shuttle.

Dropping

You'll probably be happy to know that this labor sign is visible proof that you're not going to end up pregnant forever. Dropping, or *lightening*, which is the medical term, means that your baby has settled head-down (you hope) in your pelvis.

Now, some people might notice for you that you've dropped, pointing out that you look "*HUUUUGE!*" or "ready to *POP!*"

(How nice of them.) Just breathe, let those comments go (or not!) and don't panic. You probably haven't gotten any bigger. What's happening is you just *look* bigger because your baby has dropped. Since your pelvis naturally tilts forward, your baby's bottom is now jutting out, front and center, accounting for that "extra" girth (and why you may no longer be able to fit into your maternity clothes).

Another way to tell if you've dropped is to see how many fingers you can lay flat in the space between the very top of your belly and your breastbone. As of now, you might only have been able to fit one or two fingers. Once your baby drops, you'll probably be able to fit more.

You may be one of the women who, until your baby drops, is short of breath and gets full quickly when eating. That's because your diaphragm, your lungs, your stomach, *and* your baby, who's now about the size of a roasting chicken, are all jockeying for space inside you. Once your little roaster moves down, freeing up some room for those useful organs and body parts, you will gratefully be able to take a deep breath and eat a full meal. That's the good news. But the bad news is you'll need to know the location of every bathroom within a five-foot radius because now your baby is leaning on your bladder.

On the other hand, you may be one of the women for whom dropping is a nonevent. You may not even notice that it's happened because you're carrying low to begin with and not having any trouble breathing or eating (although you'll still be looking for that bathroom every five seconds). Of course, there's the chance that your baby doesn't really drop until you're in labor and perhaps pushing, which is often the case with women who've had other babies.

Labor Signs Within Days of Delivery

What comes your way out of the next group of labor signs is pretty much a crap shoot. You might have a few of them. You might have all of them. Or you might not have *any* of them apart from contractions. And having these signs doesn't *always* mean you're in labor. They're a good indication, however, that you will soon be in labor, although how soon is anyone's guess. Just remember, no one has ever *stayed* pregnant!

Losing Your Mucus Plug

This is probably as good a time as ever to introduce your mucus plug. Your mucus plug seals off your cervix, preventing germs from getting to your baby. It's kind of like flypaper for bacteria. You might notice, in the days before you're due, that you feel crampy or uncomfortable. What's happening is your Braxton Hicks contractions are starting to work on your cervix, thinning it out (effacement) and opening it up (dilation). All this activity can cause your plug to dislodge, either in stages or all at once.

So how can you tell if you've lost your plug? You may not even notice. Or, you may find that your everyday discharge gets thicker. Maybe there's even more of it (as if that's possible!). If your plug comes out in one fell swoop, you might be wondering just what it is you're looking at. So here's the deal: your plug is viscous, like thick discharge, maybe blood-tinged, about the circumference of the tip of your pinky, and about an inch and a half long. You can lose it a little bit at a time or all at once. If you do lose your plug all at once in the toilet, be aware that once it hits the water it will expand. So, no, it's not your kidney; it's just your mucus plug. *Moving right along . . .*

Spotting

As your cervix dilates and thins out, some of its tiny capillaries can rupture, tingeing whatever discharge you're having with some blood. Internal exams at the end of pregnancy can also cause spotting. Now spotting means just that, spotting. It's not like having a heavy period, so call your doctor or midwife immediately if that seems to be happening. But just be forewarned that sometimes the spotting, when it's diluted by your discharge *and* toilet water, may seem to you like way too much bleeding. If you're at all panicked, don't hesitate to call your doctor or midwife for some peace of mind.

Diarrhea

Now that we're on really intimate terms, let's move on to your bowels. Another sign that labor may be starting is frequent, loose bowel movements or diarrhea. For example, if you normally go to the bathroom once a day and suddenly your lower back starts to feel achy as if you're getting your period, your Braxton Hicks contractions start to hurt, and you've pooped five times in the last two hours—something's going on. As unappealing as all this may seem, it might help to know that there's really brilliance in it. It's nature's way of cleaning you out to make room for your baby to pass through.

■ The Poop Scoop

You might actually be praying for this sign if it means that you're not going to "poop on the table." This is a very common fear for lots of women and it can even hold you back from pushing effectively. So if you are worried that, in addition to a baby, you might also push out whatever is left in your bowels, first of all, that's hardly anything, and second of all, it's actually good news. It means that you're pushing the right way. Just know it means nothing to the hospital staff, and you will probably not even realize it happened. When you're pushing another human being out of your body, the truth is your mind is probably on one thought and one thought only—"there are too many people in my body and somebody's got to go."

Water Breaking

You might be surprised to know that labor won't always begin with your water breaking. In actuality, less than 15 percent of labors start this way (that's one out of every five or six women). It doesn't hurt when your water breaks, although the contraction that causes it could be uncomfortable, and it can happen in one of two ways: an undeniable gush or a slow trickle.

> You might be surprised to know that less than 15 percent of labors start with your water breaking (that's one out of every five or six women).

"The Gush"

Here's your worst nightmare. You're standing in line at the grocery store, tormenting yourself by looking at a magazine spread of the glorious celebrity of the moment. She had her baby, what you thought was two days ago, and already she's back in her yoga pants and wearing a sexy, clingy gown at the Golden Globes. As you mentally try to calculate how long ago she gave birth, you suddenly feel a river of something warm and wet flowing down your legs, drenching your pants and shoes and leaving you completely mortified and standing in a puddle.

The truth be told, if your water does break in public, one look at your pregnant belly is the only clue anyone will need. Although you may not be able to protect your dignity, you can protect yourself and, if it happens at home, your bed. Stow a towel or sanitary pads in the car so you can clean up if your water breaks while you're away from home because you will keep on leaking amniotic fluid until your baby is born. At home, you can use the very same crib protector that you may have already bought for the nursery to protect your mattress. Just put it under your bottom sheet in the weeks before you're due.

"The Trickle"

Sometimes, instead of a gush of amniotic fluid, you might experience a trickle, and that scenario may be more complicated to figure out. For example, you're at work and you go to the bathroom for the millionth time that day. But when you go back to your desk, you still feel damp. So you go back to the bathroom and wipe again. On your third or fourth trip within the hour, during which you're debating whether, along with not having a stitch of clothing left that fits you and not being able to sleep because you just can't get comfortable, you now have to come to terms with the notion that you've lost control of your bladder. While it's possible you might be leaking urine, it's more likely that you're leaking amniotic fluid. When the leak is up high, the baby acts like a cork and slows down the flow to a trickle.

Whether you experience a gush or a trickle, it's now time to call your doctor or midwife. Once the amniotic membrane is no longer intact, the possibility for infection exists. He or she will want to know if the amniotic fluid is clear, pale yellow, or has a brownish-green tinge to it. If it is brownish-green, there's meconium in it and that leads us to a conversation about your *baby's* bowels. The presence of meconium means that your baby has had its first bowel movement inside of you. Your practitioner will want you to go to the hospital to get on the fetal monitor just to make sure your baby isn't being stressed by labor.

If the fluid is clear, depending on your physician's practice style, you'll either be at home or in the hospital waiting for contractions to start. Some practitioners will want to induce labor if it hasn't started within twelve to twenty-four hours, and some may even want to induce sooner. Then there are those who may go even longer, maybe twenty-four to thirty-six hours, as long as there's no sign of infection. (Remember, if you have specific preferences about induction if your water breaks, the time for making them known is well in advance of labor and delivery. See Chapter 3 for how to find out if your practitioner's practice style meets your needs.) If you're home, you can shower if you feel like it, but most practitioners will advise you not to sit in the tub because bacteria can get to your baby through the ruptured sac. Tampons may also introduce bacteria, so use a sanitary pad instead.

Contractions

Contractions can sometimes be a little tricky. Although they're often seen as the be-all and end-all of labor signs—the thought being once you start having them you're on your way—that's not always the case. You might have regular contractions for a good five hours and then all of sudden they disappear and don't come back for days. Or, you might spend an entire twenty-four hours with contractions coming eight to ten minutes apart before they finally break past the five-minute marker.

So just what will those long-awaited contractions feel like? They're different for everyone. In the early stages of labor you may feel a tightening or a little twinge that then goes away. Or, you may feel crampy, like you're getting your period. You might register that feeling for a split second and then forget about it. But after some time, you might begin to notice that what you're feeling is uncomfortable. That's when pregnant women do "the something's going on here" stare. You stop, tilt your head, and squint inwardly. Suddenly you realize, something *is* going on here.

As time goes on and your contractions continue to build, you might feel as if they begin from your lower back and wrap around to your front. You might feel them just in the front, down low; you might feel them in your legs; or you might not be able to pinpoint a specific area—all you know is that you feel them. And the way you know your labor is in gear is that your contractions keep coming back.

Eventually, the contractions might start to feel painful. The pain of contractions is different from other pain. It doesn't just come on and stay there. It's like a wave that starts, climbs, peaks, and then subsides. Then there's a rest period until it begins again. That rest period is what gives you the breathing space you need to get ready for the next contraction.

Your doctor or midwife will want you to call when you have regular contractions, meaning they become more and more frequent

---

▪ Labor: True or "False"?

You may have three nights of contractions between 2 A.M. and 5 A.M. every morning for three mornings in a row before labor finally kicks in. You may have full-blown contractions and get to the hospital and suddenly they disappear (remember that "fight-or-flight" response?). You may be told that what you're feeling is "false" labor. But if you've been gripping your partner's hand with each contraction, it certainly doesn't feel "false" to you.

You're not considered in what's officially called active labor until your contractions come consistently and regularly and your cervix reaches three to four centimeters. But whatever you're feeling before you get to that point, isn't in your head. It's *your* body's way of getting ready for labor—kind of like a car engine that needs some time to warm up before it turns over. So whatever you may be told, rest assured, there's nothing "false" about it. Something is definitely happening. It's just that labor hasn't fully kicked in.

---

and their intensity grows. Interpret those instructions according to what *you* need. You may need some help figuring out if what you're feeling *are* contractions. You may need feedback to get a feeling for where you are in your labor. Or, you may just want your practitioner to know you're in labor, even if it's early on, because it helps you to know that they know.

Once you get in touch with your doctor or midwife, he or she will want to know how often your contractions are coming and how long they're lasting. To tell how often they're coming, time your contractions from the beginning of one to the beginning of the next. To tell how long each one lasts, time the same contraction from its beginning to its end.

The formula for when to think about leaving for the hospital generally goes like this: when your contractions are coming every five minutes, each lasting close to a minute, and that's been going on for an hour or two.

Don't worry about timing them continuously. You're not going to miss your cue that it's time to leave for the hospital. During your prenatal visits, you've very likely had a conversation with your doctor about when to start thinking about leaving for the hospital. For first-time moms, that formula generally goes like this: when your contractions are coming every five minutes, each lasting close to a minute, and that's been going on for an hour or two. If you've given birth before, you might be instructed to call a bit earlier (when your contractions are coming every five to seven minutes). Each practitioner has his or her own version of this formula. Some may look at it as the time to touch base, if you haven't already. Others may look at it as the time to come into the office to be checked or to go to the hospital. It could take some time to reach that point because most labors, especially the first time around, tend to build slowly, and you'll notice when things start to feel different. If, however, your contractions start out at three to five minutes apart, don't wait for them to "spread out." Your uterus is working faster, and you'll end up leaving for the hospital sooner. Remember, you're not out there on your own trying to figure this out. Call your doctor, midwife, and/or doula.

A good rule of thumb is to time your contractions to get a sense of their rhythm and then when you feel a change—maybe they're more intense or picking up speed—time them again. Another option is to time them and then try to ignore them if you can until you get to a point where you can't. Then go ahead and time them again. Remember, even if your contractions aren't at the "prescribed" interval but you feel like you need to call—*for whatever reason*—then just call.

· 6 ·

Labor: How It Works

When it gets down to the nitty-gritty of describing labor, much of what you'll hear sounds like it comes straight out of a medical textbook. Progress is measured numerically: in centimeters; in sixty-second contractions; in minutes between contractions. The whole process is divided into distinct phases and stages, including early labor, active labor, transition, and delivery. And when you're in labor, your body is very busy doing important-sounding things that maybe you never even knew it *could* do until you took childbirth classes, things like "dilate" and "efface."

Tossing the Textbook

All this tidy terminology might lure you into believing that labor is quite orderly. But the truth is labors don't read a medical textbook. In fact, they're pretty much all over the page. Your best friend's labor could come on like gangbusters, unexpectedly announcing itself with a gush of water and contractions starting at five minutes apart. *Your* labor could start out languidly, with contractions taking their own sweet time to build, maybe over a span of hours or even days.

One of the many incredible things about childbirth is that even with all the medical advances in our lifetime we don't exactly know what triggers the moment when labor begins. It could be the baby. It could be the uterus. But nobody can *really* say. Every labor has its own unique magic and its own story, unfolding in its own way.

That's why the traditional, cookie-cutter description of labor can be a misleading one. Stack after stack of birth books pay homage to that "tried-and-true" standard, paying lip service to the fact that every labor is different. Well, as you know by now, this entire book is pretty much devoted to the fact that every labor is different, as is each and every laboring woman. Applying a ready-made childbirth formula to your labor experience just doesn't work.

> Every labor has its own unique magic and its own story, unfolding in its own way.

The plain truth is, there's really no telling when your labor will start, how long it will last, what it will be like, and how it will feel. If your reaction to that is "that's not going to work for me so let's schedule an induction right now," may we remind you there's plenty that you *do* know. For example, you might be a real homebody. You're out of sorts in a hotel room let alone a hospital room. You might feel best laboring at home for as long as you're comfortable. And when you do go to the hospital, bringing some familiar things with you—your pillows and favorite throw or blanket, for instance—can make a big difference.

Now, you might think, OK, that *feels* right, but let's cut to the chase here. Exactly *how* does this help the baby come out? Because isn't that the point of all this? What about the "hee-hee-hoo-hoo" breathing and the different labor positions? As we said earlier, you won't find those here. Not because they don't work, but because unless they fit you and you feel comfortable doing them, they *won't* work. The best thing you can do in labor is to be yourself. And you do that by tuning in to what you know about yourself and how you're feeling in the moment. Then you'll be able to do what *you* need to do as you follow your labor wherever it goes.

Labor and Delivery:
The "User-Friendly" Version

So, physiologically speaking, here's how labor and delivery work. If you have the ability to read about the way the body works in a book and can actually visualize it in your head, this next section is right up your alley. If, on the other hand, no matter how hard you try, these kinds of descriptions make absolutely no sense at all to you ("now *where* is my uterus?"), you may feel like skipping this section. Go right ahead. But we promise, we've made this as user-friendly as you'll probably ever see it.

The "Stars" of the Labor and Delivery Show

Meet your uterus and cervix—the "stars" of labor and delivery. First let's talk about your uterus. Believe it or not, your uterus is mostly muscle. In the "muscle strength" hall of fame, this amazing organ gets pretty high marks. That's pretty impressive *and* reassuring. Because it's the contractions of these very capable uterine muscles that help get your baby out of your body. In order to get an idea of what your uterus looks like, it might help to picture it this way. Think of your uterus and cervix as the shape of an upside-down wine bottle that's squat and round. The round part of the bottle is the uterus. The part where the neck *meets* the bottle is the cervix—the outlet through which your baby will emerge. The neck of the bottle is your vaginal canal (aka the birth canal).

Now instead of being made of glass, transform this bottle in your mind into something soft and stretchy, like a turtleneck sweater. The cervix is the turtleneck part. During your pregnancy your cervix is long and thick, tight, and closed in order to keep the baby in.

But here's what happens in labor. What you actually feel when you're having contractions is your *uterus* contracting. Your uterus is flexing its muscle power, tightening up like a bicep because it's pulling at your cervix, which has started to soften and thin out. That's effacement. Once the cervix is soft and thin enough, your uterine contractions are able to start spreading your cervix open. That's dilation. Effacement and dilation go hand and hand. This thinning and spreading continues until your cervix is pulled all the way back by your baby's ears (think of that soft, stretchy turtleneck being pulled back over your baby's head). When your cervix has reached that point, you are typically ten centimeters dilated. How long does it take to get to that point? The timing is different for everyone, but in first labors progress is usually slow until your cervix gets to four to five centimeters. In fact, getting to that point could take hours or even days. But once you reach four to five centimeters, your labor usually turns a corner and will very likely pick up speed.

Now, if we may, let's just take a moment to clear up any confusion you may be experiencing about the pronunciation of the word *centimeter*. You may have noticed that people in the medical profession often pronounce it "*son*-timeter." This may cause you to wonder: A. Is this some kind of secret password to a club of which you're clearly not a member? B. Are you and your doctor speaking the same language? or C. Have you been pronouncing it wrong your whole life?

Let it be known that a "*son*-timeter" is the same thing as a "*cen*-timeter." The pronunciation is simply a carryover from the French. And, no matter how you say it, you still need to get to *ten* of them in order to give birth. A little rusty when it comes to the metric system? Ten centimeters equal four inches (if you've gotten up to get your tape measure, you may want to check that out sitting down).

Pushing, Pushing . . .

Once your uterus has pulled your cervix completely back and out of the way, it can now start pushing your baby *down* and out through your pelvis. And push it does. Once your baby's head is low enough to press on your rectum, generally you can't help but want to push.

Nature's wise like that. So there you are, you and your uterus pushing together to move your baby down and out.

There is this other person involved, your baby, who plays just as much of a role. It is a duet—unlike any other.

Once your baby's born and breathing on its own, your placenta gets a signal that it's no longer needed. It peels away from the uterine wall and your uterus pushes it out. So if you're thinking, "Great, after all that, now I have to push something *else* out of my body?," not to worry, your uterus does the job for you. You may have to bear down a little to help, but compared to having to push a seven- to nine-pound human being out of your body, your soft placenta, which weighs one and a half to two pounds, feels like a breeze.

That's how labor and delivery work. On paper. But that's only part of the story. Those are the mechanics. What's missing is *you* and all the details—big, little, and in-between—that make it *your* story: how long or short your labor is, how it feels for you physically and emotionally, what you're doing, and how you're doing. But don't forget, it's not just about you. There is this other person involved, your baby, who plays just as much of a role. It is a duet—unlike any other.

· 7 ·

Labor at Home

Now that you have an idea of what your body's doing in labor and delivery, it's time to put you into the equation. Let's talk about what *you're* doing. The remaining chapters will take you through all of labor and delivery—from the moment you realize you're in labor to the birth of your baby. They'll help you get a feel for what will be right for you each step of the way. We'll start by discussing what labor might look like *before* you go to the hospital.

How It Usually Begins: Early Labor

According to the textbook, you may be in early labor when your contractions are ten to twenty minutes apart and they last for thirty to forty-five seconds. During early labor your cervix will dilate to three centimeters. OK. That's all very clear and concise. But here's the thing about early labor that may not be: some early labors can be pretty sneaky. You may not even realize you were in early labor until you're actually through it. Or, your water could break with contractions setting in immediately, closing in much faster than ten minutes apart. Forget about "crampy," these contractions are way beyond that. Then there are those labors that are so by the book that you were able to zero in on that very first contraction and have been timing them on and off ever since. You just never know.

What You Can Do in Early Labor

So let's say you realize you're in early labor, you've alerted your doctor or midwife, and now you're at home waiting it out. What are you doing? You may be tempted to pull out that stopwatch and start timing your contractions if you haven't done so already. If you're dying to see what stage your contractions are at, then by all means, have a look at the stopwatch. Then do yourself a favor and put it away. Chronicling every element of your labor isn't medically necessary and may only make you feel frustrated because most early labors come on very gradually. It could take some time before your labor is in full swing. The best time to take that stopwatch out again is when your contractions are so regular and persistent that you can no longer ignore them.

What else are you doing? You've probably been given advice such as "Just keep walking to get your labor going." So maybe you're considering doing laps around your local mall. You might be thinking of running out to do some last-minute shopping. Perhaps you're horrified that you didn't get in that last-minute waxing or pedicure. It's our opinion that unless you want to burn out at the beginning (or you won't labor as well with hairy legs), the best thing you can do for yourself is not to overdo it.

That being said, pacing yourself, fueling, and hydrating are pretty tried-and-true ways to give your early labor the best opportunity to progress *and* shore up your stamina. The following ideas are meant to be interpreted according to your personality and how you're feeling at the time. You may be to the right or left of them, or smack-dab in the center. So if you're worried that all of a sudden we've turned into the "labor police," we haven't. Translate everything we're talking about into what works for you.

Pace Yourself

It's a really good strategy to conserve your energy and pace yourself because how long you'll be in labor is anybody's guess. If it's nighttime, try to stay in bed and rest or sleep between contractions. If you can't stay in bed, be restful in a way that works for you. Hang out on the couch or in a rocking chair. Watch TV, read, flip through magazines. Take a long bath or, if your water has broken, just a shower. (Remember, there is a risk of bacteria getting to your baby through your ruptured amniotic sac if you sit in the tub.)

Pacing yourself, fueling, and hydrating are pretty tried-and-true ways to give your early labor the best opportunity to progress *and* shore up your stamina.

If it's daytime, do the same thing. If you're the type who finds it hard to just take it easy and instead feels best when you're out and about, take a leisurely walk around your neighborhood instead of doing a mini-marathon at the mall. Go to your local nail place for a manicure or pedicure instead of running all over town taking care of last-minute errands. If you feel best in your own "nest" but are going a little stir crazy waiting for your labor to pick up, do a final futzing around in your baby's room to make sure everything's in order or write down what you're feeling in your baby's birth book. The point is you really need to be taking care of *you* so you're not so exhausted that you're completely depleted by the time your labor really gets going.

Think Drinks

Here's another thing to consider as you wait for your labor to kick in: bodies that are fueled and hydrated tend to labor better than bodies that are starved and dehydrated. So, if you can stomach it, think about eating and drinking something. Here are some guidelines that may be helpful: liquids are easier to get down than solids, eating or drinking slowly is better than quickly, and, when it comes to how much, a little is better than a lot.

Hydrate, hydrate, hydrate. Sip water or, if you feel queasy, ginger ale. If it appeals to you, consider making yourself a smoothie. Blend up some milk, yogurt, and a banana. The combination of protein and carbohydrates can sustain you during labor. However, if just the thought of a smoothie makes you nauseous, then don't have one. And if you never drink smoothies, labor probably isn't the time to start. Remember, do what feels right for you. That's what works.

Snack on Carbohydrates

Any athlete will tell you that "carbo-loading" is the way to prepare for an endurance event (and we think labor pretty much falls into that category). That's because complex carbs found in pasta, cereal, and whole-grain toast or bagels are a great source of stored energy. It's good to have some of that energy in reserve because once you get to the hospital you won't be allowed to eat.

But instead of "loading" carbs, eat lightly so you're not digesting a heavy meal during labor. If you're in the early stages of labor and it's dinnertime, maybe eat some pasta—but without the tomato sauce. Spicy or acidic foods can set your stomach off, especially once you move into active labor. If you don't have an appetite, maybe nibble on some whole-grain crackers, toast, or cereal.

Some practitioners may ask you to switch to clear fluids once your contractions are regular and really uncomfortable, coming every five minutes. That means liquids you can see through, like water, ginger ale, or non-citrus fruit juice. It's a good idea to dilute fruit juice with water or seltzer to avoid nausea. Food tends to just sit in your stomach once your labor gets going, and that can cause heartburn or nausea.

Careful Calling Versus Phone Blasting

Once you know that you really are in labor, the thought of it might get you pretty revved up. In the midst of your excitement, you might be tempted to call everyone you know to tell them the news. But before you pick up that phone, think again. If your labor decides to take its sweet old time and you're hours away from leaving for the hospital, do you really want all those people checking back in with you to ask, "What's going on? Have you had the baby yet? What are you doing *home*?" Trust us on this one; they will keep calling and you won't want to keep talking.

If you're ready to share the news, just be judicious about those you share it with. Maybe set up some personal boundaries. Tell those you do call that you'd rather they not keep checking in. You'll call *them* when there's anything to report.

Assess Your Baggage

Another thing you can do in early labor, depending on how you feel, of course, is to get your hospital bag in order. In addition to the things you need for you and your baby, there are some other things you may want to consider tucking in. Just having them can help make your hospital room feel more like your comfort zone. Remember, the safer and more at ease you feel, the more effectively you'll be able to labor.

Familiar Things to Bring
- Your own pillows—they smell like you and home (That's what makes them great for under your head and to wrap

yourself around when you're lying on your side. You can use the very thin hospital pillows between your legs or behind your back for support. Just put colored or printed cases on *your* pillows so they don't get lost in the hospital laundry.)

- A blanket or throw that you love—to spread over the (very thin) hospital-issue blankets
- An oversized T-shirt and robe to labor in if you don't want to wear the hospital gown
- Your favorite comfy socks in case you feel chilly
- Slippers or shoes that are easy to slip into and out of should you want to walk around the hospital floor
- A bathing suit if you're modest and think you might want to labor in the shower or tub
- Flip-flops if you have a thing about strange bathroom floors
- Hair bands, barrettes—whatever you use to pull your hair back
- Lip balm
- Your favorite CDs or tapes—if music is important to you—along with something to play them on

For Your Spouse or Partner

- Layers, layers, layers. *You* might need the thermostat turned down low because you're hot, but to the average person *not* in labor, the room could feel like Alaska. And vice versa. You might be freezing and need the thermostat turned up high, and now your spouse or partner is in the Sahara. Layers will allow your spouse or partner to peel off or bundle up according to the temperature.
- A bathing suit, flip-flops, shorts, or spare set of clothes so your spouse or partner won't have to stay in damp clothing after helping you labor in the shower
- Food, food, and more food to keep your partner or spouse fueled while he supports you through your labor. (The

■ A Note to Your Spouse or Partner

You've probably figured out by now that your wife or partner is going to be pretty busy once labor kicks in. You may be wondering what exactly it is that you're going to be doing. Are you supposed to turn into the "ultimate" labor coach, timing each contraction as you guide her through breathing exercises? Then, when it's time for the baby to be born, maybe suggest some different pushing positions?

We're here to tell you that you don't have to be anyone except who you really are. Whether you're at home or at the hospital, the best thing you can do for your spouse or partner is support her the way you always have—whether that means rubbing her feet, making her laugh, or staying close by or not quite so close by. Don't worry, she'll let you know if what you're doing isn't working.

There might be times during labor when you feel pretty helpless and that's pretty much how it is. It's really hard to be in the presence of someone working through pain and not be able to fix it—especially someone you love. After all, you're not feeling what she's feeling and, for the most part, you're dependent on her for cues as to what she needs and where she is in her labor. Sometimes the only thing you'll be able to do for her is to just be there. That might seem like a small job compared to what she's going through, but it's the biggest part of what you can do.

One last bit of advice. If you both have different opinions or expectations about labor and delivery, they should be ironed out way in advance. The delivery room is not the place for conflicting agendas. You really need to feel like you're working together as a team. It may help to keep in mind that, ultimately, she's the one going through this momentous physical and emotional experience of giving birth. So if she has a strong need to do it one way (i.e., *not* have your mother in the delivery room), it's important that her needs and wishes be respected.

typical hospital fare available after hours—Jell-O, saltines, and soda—just doesn't cut it. Pack whatever snacks and sandwiches you usually eat and bring food for yourself for *after* delivery. Chances are you'll be ravenous, and you'll have exactly what you want right there [you'll really thank us for this one!].)

It's really hard to be in the presence of someone working through pain and not be able to fix it—especially someone you love.

What You Can Do at Home as Your Labor Progresses

Keep in mind that these labor tools can be recycled if need be. One may work for five minutes and then you might need to move on to a few more. Some time later you may go back to the one you used two hours ago. Or, you might just find that there is that one magic thing that works for you throughout your entire labor. You'll know what feels right.

- **Be a couch potato.** If you're feeling overwhelmed and need some distraction, curl up on the couch and turn on the TV or radio. Get under a soft blanket and zone in and out between contractions.

- **Get on the ball.** If your contractions are picking up and you feel the urge to move through them, roll forward and back on your birth ball, sway from side to side, and/or do gentle bounces during your contractions. Place your ball near a bed or couch stacked with pillows so you can drape yourself over them, Raggedy Ann–style, and rest once your contraction is over. If you don't like the ball's "rubber-y" smell, cover it with a soft blanket (there are even aromatherapy birth ball covers if you're so inclined).

- **Rock-a-bye, baby.** The restful movement of a rocking chair or baby glider might be just what you need to soothe your contractions, especially if staying still isn't working for you. Sit on and surround yourself with soft pillows (behind your back and head, under your arms, over your belly) and rock gently through your contractions. The rocking motion can even help your baby navigate the different diameters of your pelvis, moving him or her down.

- **Get off my back.** If you're having back labor (contractions that feel like they're entirely focused in your lower back, often due to your baby's position), try these forward-leaning positions that can move your baby off your back.

  - If you feel better lying down, lie on your side and tilt forward a bit so the weight of your belly is on the bed or pillows.
  - Get on all fours, either on the bed or on the floor, with pillows or blankets under your knees and sway from side to side.
  - Sit on a birth ball while leaning over a chair or the bed, letting your belly hang.

  Try heating pads or ice packs on your back, depending on what feels best. Try acupressure—your spouse or partner can apply firm finger pressure just below the center of the ball of your foot. What can be really effective is having someone press the heel of his or her hand into the small of your back. A substitute for this (when that person's arm is falling off) is to put a tennis ball on your bed and lean back into it.

- **Get into the "birth spa" zone.** With the help of your spouse, partner, and/or doula, create a soothing, spalike oasis to labor in at home. Let your support team guide you into the tub or shower and sit on a towel-covered birth ball (make sure there's a towel underneath it to prevent the ball from sliding). You'll need a towel wrapped around your belly and back and one around your shoulders. Water is then poured or sprayed over the towels to keep them warm or at whatever temperature you like. For a reviving "labor-aid," freeze lemonade in ice trays beforehand so you can suck on the lemony cubes while you're in the "spa." When you're ready to come out, wrap up in a cozy flannel sheet that's been warmed in the dryer—that feels like Nirvana. This can be replicated in the hospital shower later on (use a flannel blanket from the hospital warmer as your towel).

When to Go to the Hospital

You've been sipping water. You munched on some toast or ate some pasta earlier on. You're packed. Your legs are as smooth as your soon-to-be baby's bottom. And now you're feeling like it just might be time to go to the hospital. But how do you know if it's *really* time?

The formula that your doctor or midwife has probably discussed with you for when to start thinking about going to the hospital generally goes like this: when your contractions come every five minutes, each one lasting around a minute, and that's been happening for one or two hours. Now that formula is helpful except for one thing. It doesn't take into account how *you're* feeling.

For example, maybe you've gotten into a rhythm that works for you at home, alternating between the tub and the birth ball. You've been having contractions at five minutes apart for almost an hour, but you're managing just fine and you live ten minutes from the hospital. Or, maybe your contractions are starting to feel pretty intense even though they're "only" eight minutes apart and that's making you nervous.

How Well Are You Laboring at Home?

Here's how you can adapt the "when to go to the hospital" formula to your own barometer for what's right for you. It begins with asking yourself the question "How well am I laboring at home?" If you feel most comfortable in your own space and want to be there as long as you safely can, you might stretch the formula a bit and stay home as long as possible. If you feel anxious at home and would rather be in a clinical setting because you want feedback and support, you may need to go in earlier than the formula advises.

Getting the Feedback You Need

Remember, you're not alone in making this decision. Whether you're feeling good or not so good at home, talk to your doctor or midwife as often as you need to. He or she can give you some perspective about where you are in your labor based on how you sound and how dilated or effaced you were at your last prenatal exam. Your contractions may very well be fitting the "when to go to the hospital formula," but there is the possibility you could still be in the early stages of labor.

Now you're bound to have heard that if you get to the hospital too early you'll be sent home (with your tail between your legs). Here's what you should know about that: if you *are* in labor, you can most certainly be admitted. If you find out that you've not progressed enough, just knowing where you are in labor may give you the relief you need to wait it out at home. And if you find out that you are in labor, but still early on, you might *choose* to go home. But if you feel you need to stay, then say so.

Here's another option for getting the feedback you need. If it's during office hours, you can always go into your doctor's or midwife's office to find out how far you have progressed (more than likely he or she will want to see you anyway to check your progress). The information you get can help you feel better about what's going on and help you plan accordingly.

Nighttime, on the other hand, can have a whole different energy to it. Knowing that your doctor's or midwife's office is closed up tight for the night could suddenly make you feel isolated and vulnerable. You can still get the feedback you need to feel better. Don't hesitate to call your doctor, midwife, or doula, if you've hired one, whatever the hour. Again, they can get a sense of where you are by listening to you go through some contractions while you're on the phone with them. They'll also get a sense of your emotional state, which is another good indicator of how far along you are.

Neither Snow, Nor Rain, Nor Rush-Hour Traffic . . .

Logistically speaking, there are some other things to factor into the "when to go to the hospital" equation.

- How far away from the hospital you live
- The weather
- Traffic

If you live a good distance away and want to spend the least amount of time possible laboring in the hospital (i.e., you live in the suburbs and the hospital where you're having your baby is in the city), as soon as you think you're in labor you might consider staying with friends or family who live closer or even getting a nearby hotel room. This accomplishes two important things. It eradicates any anxiety you may have over getting to the hospital "in time" *and* it allows you to labor in the way you need to labor—if that means being out of the hospital environment.

Another option, if you live a good distance away and you know you'll feel more secure in your hospital room for the duration of your labor, is to consider leaving for the hospital soon after you think you're in labor. This will wipe away any worries you might have about being close to delivery but far from the hospital. Be in touch with your doctor or midwife to work out a lead time that you both feel comfortable with.

As you consider the "when to go to the hospital" question, be sure to add to that equation the possibilities of bad weather conditions and traffic issues. Waiting for the car to be shoveled out and then getting stuck behind a salt truck is going to increase the time it takes for you to get to the hospital, as will bumper-to-bumper rush-hour traffic. Staying one step ahead of weather and traffic will give you peace of mind.

When Labor Has the Last Word

The question, "How will I know when it's time to go to the hospital?" is really one of the "waiting for baby" biggies. On the anxiety-producing scale, it's probably in a dead heat with "How will I know I'm in labor?" Not only is it a biggie for you, it's also a biggie for your spouse or partner who, whether or not he or she is saying it, very likely feels a huge responsibility to get you there "in time." That's why calling your doctor or midwife for feedback can help. So don't hesitate to pick up the phone.

In an effort to set up some signposts in this never-before-traveled terrain, it's tempting to let the general formula—"When your contractions have been five minutes apart, lasting around a minute, for at least an hour . . ."—become your mantra. While it can be a helpful guide, keep in mind that some labors defy the way things "typically" go.

Tanya: My water breaking at about 2 A.M. woke me up right away. I stumbled out of bed and into the bathroom to clean up. And then about a half hour later, just as my husband was putting the wet sheets into the washing machine, my contractions really kicked in. They were so intense and kept on coming that I was really thrown for a loop. My husband kind of jolted into action and started timing them. He told me they were about four minutes apart, and I said, "No way!" I had it in my head that my contractions would come on slowly and it would probably take a long time before they started coming every five minutes. I knew from my doctor and everything that I'd read, that that's when I'd go to the hospital—when my contractions were five minutes apart. Now here were mine at four.

Formulas and advice can help, but nothing takes the place of listening to yourself and listening to your labor.

When labor comes on like gangbusters as it did for Tanya, it can take you by complete surprise. There goes that birth script right out the window. All those things you pictured you'd be doing and the way you figured you'd be feeling while waiting for your labor to pick up speed are history. You might be left without your bearings and feeling like your "story" is being rewritten, without any input from you.

Tanya: I really don't know what I was thinking. That my contractions would all of a sudden slow down to five minutes apart? It was when I had to get on my hands and knees in the middle of a really strong contraction that my husband said, "We're out of here!" An hour after I got to the hospital I started pushing, and Vanessa came out like a firecracker. And she's been that way ever since! Never in a million years did I think that that was how it would happen for me.

The moral of every labor story is: every labor is different. Formulas and labor tips may help you more than you ever thought they could. Or, they may not be at all applicable to what you're going through. In the weeks and days leading up to labor, you might have an idea of what you think will be right for you, but it's important to stay flexible. Once you're actually in labor, you may find out that you need to leave for the hospital on the early side of the formula. *The very early side.* Or, you may find out that you'd rather leave on the late side. You may not even have a choice in the matter. Forget about that labor story you wrote in your head. Your contractions are calling and they're saying it's time to go. Which leads to another moral: formulas and advice can help, but nothing takes the place of listening to yourself and listening to your labor.

· 8 ·

Labor in the Hospital

You've made the decision that it's time to go. Or, maybe your labor made the decision for you. Whatever the case, making your way to the hospital might feel pretty monumental. You're closing the door on one chapter of your life and opening up another, and it may all of a sudden hit you that you're really on your way to having a baby.

Getting There

You may have time to slowly and calmly get you and all your stuff from the house to the car. But if your contractions are coming hard and fast, it could wind up feeling like an episode of "I Love Lucy." If it's doable, think about loading the car early on in your labor (and make sure you keep enough gas in the car to get to the hospital!).

Depending on how quickly your contractions are coming and how strong they are, it may be hard to get comfortable in the car. If you've been moving around during your labor, being in the car may make you feel claustrophobic. On top of everything else you're feeling, if your spouse or partner is nervous about getting you to the hospital quickly, it may feel like you're on one wild ride. Leaving for the hospital while your contractions are still manageable can make the difference between a car ride that's panicky and one that's not.

To make your transition to the hospital as smooth as possible, here are some things you can find out and do ahead of time.

Good Birth Savvy: Things to Know and Do Before You Leave for the Hospital

- In case you arrive at the hospital after visiting hours are over, find out in advance which entrance to use and where to park. Many hospitals route patients through the emergency room entrance after hours. Be sure to keep in mind that if you park in the emergency room parking lot, it's possible that your spouse or partner may have to come back down and move your car at some point.

- Check to see if valet parking is available. Some hospitals offer it, although probably not at 2 A.M.

- Once you're parked, keep in mind that if you leave something in the car, you probably won't go down to get it until after your baby is born. So take with you anything that you'll need for labor, including your CD player, birth ball, snacks, and so on. You may want to pack a labor bag and a separate postpartum bag if there's too much stuff for one trip. Someone can always come back down for the second bag after the delivery.

- Find out if the hospital where you're delivering sends out preadmitting forms. You'll be doing yourself a big favor if you fill them out beforehand. This way, at the height of a contraction, you won't have to recall your Social Security number or rummage through your purse for your insurance card (although do have it on hand anyway).

- If someone does happen to ask you for admitting information during a really hard contraction, wait for it to subside before you answer. After all, you're hard at work. (No one asks Venus or Serena Williams when they're at match point on the tennis court to stop and recite *their* phone numbers.)

- If you're offered a wheelchair and you feel like you need it, then take it. If it's better for you to keep walking, then don't.

In Your Room

After you make it through Admitting, your next stop is the Labor & Delivery floor. Your doctor or midwife will have called ahead so the staff knows to expect you. Once you're there you'll meet your nurse and she'll take you to your labor and delivery room (which will be private, although the room that you get after your baby is born may not be, depending on how full Labor & Delivery is and your insurance coverage). Your nurse will begin a bevy of questions and procedures. This is where you'll begin to get a sense of the chemistry you'll have with her. For example, if you're not able to respond because you're at the height of a contraction, your nurse's awareness, respect, and patience will be another indicator of how you'll fare with her.

The routine can vary from hospital to hospital, but here's generally what happens. Your nurse will offer you a plastic bag marked "Patient's Belongings" (which may cause you to wonder, "Am I having a baby, doing time, or both?"). She'll provide you with the hospital nightgown that you can put on if you want, or you *can* choose to wear your own T-shirt or nightgown. She may have you give a urine sample and ask you to get into the bed to take your vital signs.

Electronic Fetal Monitoring

The next thing your nurse will do is put you on the fetal monitor for about half an hour in order to see how your baby is doing. Monitoring is traditionally done while you're lying in bed because that's the best position for the nurse when it comes to adjusting the belts and locating the baby's heart rate. If you're comfortable in bed, stay there. But if that's not a good position for you, let her know. Your nurse and support team can work with you to figure out alternative lying or standing positions that are better for you—for example, lying on your side supported by pillows, sitting in a rocking chair or on your birth ball, or standing and draping your arms and upper body over a stack of pillows on your raised hospital bed so you can do little knee bends or rock and sway with the contractions.

The fetal monitor has two monitoring devices—one picks up the intensity of your contractions and the other tracks your baby's heart rate. If you move around a lot, the monitors (which are held in place by either two belts or a belly band, both made of soft, stretchy material) can shift, particularly the one that picks up the baby's heart rate, which is lower down. So if you need to change positions, your nurse, spouse, partner, or doula can hold the fetal monitor in place so you're in a comfortable position for you and the monitor is where the nurse needs it to be in order to get a reading. Some nurses will even show you (or whoever is with you) how to unplug from the monitor and then re-plug, just in case you have to get up to use the bathroom.

> If you're comfortable in bed, stay there. But if that's not a good position for you, your nurse and support team can work with you to figure out alternative lying or standing positions that are better.

After this initial monitoring, many practitioners feel comfortable with intermittent monitoring. If it's important to you to be monitored only when "necessary," talk to your practitioner about that ahead of time. There's usually room for compromise in the earlier stages of labor if everything is OK. The closer you are to delivery, the more continuous the monitoring typically.

▪ Position Options During Monitoring

If the thought of being attached to a monitor makes you feel more like a prisoner than a patient and/or lying back doesn't feel good during your contractions, here are some alternatives to consider:

- **If you're most comfortable in bed:** Try lying on your side hugging your pillows with additional pillows between your legs and behind your back. Another option is to kneel on your bed, draping yourself over a stack of pillows and the raised head of the bed.
- **If you're most comfortable out of the bed:** Stand rocking or swaying while draped over pillows that have been piled high on your raised hospital bed. Or, try rocking in a rocking chair with pillows behind your back, under you, and cushioning your arms. Many women just naturally rock in labor. It's instinct. If there's not a rocker in your room, someone with you or one of the staff can bring one over from the newborn nursery or patient's lounge.

The objective of all these gymnastics is twofold: that you can do what you need to do, which is to labor comfortably and effectively, *and* that the nurse can do what she needs to do—get a reading of your baby's heart rate.

Intravenous (IV)

Now that you're in the hospital, traditionally you won't be allowed solid food. But you will get ice chips (wow), ginger ale (yippee), or maybe, if you're really, really lucky, Italian ice (yahoo!). Depending on what you and your practitioner have decided in advance, an IV may or may not be started at this time. IVs prevent dehydration; they hydrate you if you haven't been able to drink fluids and/or you've been vomiting; and they get medicine, should you need it, into your bloodstream quickly. If needles make you nervous or you want to be able to shower in labor, make it a point to discuss that with your practitioner in advance of labor. He or she might be willing to forgo an IV if there's not an absolute need for one.

But if your practitioner feels strongly that you have an IV, a great way to accommodate each other's needs is the heparin lock—the part of the IV that goes into your arm, minus the tubing. The heparin lock can also be a good alternative if you're taking a "wait-and-see approach" to getting an epidural. Most anesthesiologists require that you have a full bag of IV fluid before getting an epidural. Having a heparin lock in place can save some time if you decide you want an epidural. If you tested positive for Group B streptococcus, while you'll need IV antibiotics at intervals throughout your labor, it can be turned into a heparin lock to give you mobility and allow you to shower if you want.

And, last but not least, if you have a history of being stuck a million times in order to get a "good" vein or you hate having your blood drawn, let your nurse know that ahead of time. If she isn't able to get your IV started after a couple attempts and/or you've reached your limit, ask for someone else who can.

Assessing Your Labor Nurse

Once all the questions have been asked and the procedures completed to formally admit you to Labor & Delivery, you'll have a good idea of whether or not you're comfortable with your nurse. The majority of labor nurses are dedicated, caring, and supportive. If you feel that your nurse is not and will have a negative impact on your labor and delivery, you really do have the option of asking for someone who might be better suited for you. Contrary to popular belief, just because you've been assigned a nurse, you don't have to stick it out with her if it's not working. Again, think of it as a win-win situation for both of you. You won't have to endure the tension and bad feelings that can come from a mismatch and neither will she.

Just as we said in Chapter 3, when it comes to making a change like this, there's more anxiety in the anticipation of it. But making the request could mean the difference between saying after your delivery, "It was fine. Our nurse wasn't so great, but the baby and I are OK." Or, "We had the greatest nurse. She even stayed past her shift to see the baby born. We couldn't have done it without her."

Your spouse or partner (or whoever you have with you who is best suited for the job) can ask for the nurse in charge and let her know that it's not working between you and your assigned nurse. Be specific about what you need more of and/or less of so she can make a better match.

The Internal Exam

An internal exam is done shortly after you're admitted in order to assess where you are in your labor. It may be your nurse, doctor, or midwife who does it, or, if you're at a teaching hospital, it may be a resident who does it. This internal exam can be a very big deal psychologically. You've been laboring at home for however long and you naturally want to see the results of all your hard work. But when it comes to finding out how dilated you are, it can feel a little bit like Olympic judging: will that judge please give you anything above a three?

Here's something very important to keep in mind. What this internal exam tells you is the status of your cervix and how low your baby's head is. What it doesn't tell you is how hard you've worked. Obviously, if you get the results you want to hear, you're going to feel good. If you don't, you might feel anywhere from disheartened to devastated. It's really hard, especially when you've been working so hard, not to see immediate results. But just know that no matter what information you get from this internal exam, anything is possible. There's no telling what your contractions and your baby are doing or going to do to your cervix and how much or how little time that may take. And actually, the piece that's most revealing about your progress is how effaced you are. The thinner your cervix is the more easily it will dilate. You could be "just" two centimeters dilated but almost completely effaced and wind up giving birth four hours later.

> No matter what information you get from the internal exam, anything is possible. There's no telling what your contractions and your baby are doing or going to do to your cervix and how much or how little time that may take.

It might help to keep your expectations in check by remembering that the longest stretch of labor tends to be from one to five centimeters. So if you're starting to feel like you're going to be in labor until next month, it's really important to try to make your way through one contraction at a time. You can always reevaluate where you are a few hours later. Have another internal exam if you need the feedback; or, if you're not ready to deal with the information, maybe you can put off the internal for a bit.

During times like this your support team can really help you keep things in perspective. How they help you navigate through how you're feeling about where you are in your labor can make a huge difference and lessen the fear that you'll be stuck where you are forever (i.e., "If it's this bad now, how am I going to deal with what's going to happen in an hour?"). Their presence and perspective can

■ **The Contraction Mantra (or Not)**

Just take it one contraction at a time. Don't think about the one that came before *or* the one that's coming. All you have to do is get through this one contraction. Be here now.

reassure you that you're doing beautifully and everything is going exactly as it should be. And if you feel that it isn't, they can help you see what options you have.

The Dating Game of Labor Coping Strategies

So how *will* you be coping with those contractions? The norm is, about eight weeks before your due date, you take a series of childbirth classes with a group of pregnant strangers and their significant others to learn just that. You might even skip the series and cram it into a weekend or single-day crash course (probably in some hotel banquet hall with *many* pregnant strangers).

> What you'll be doing to cope with contractions depends entirely on your unique mix of temperament, personality, likes, dislikes, and desires.

What do you get to show for that effort? You get your breathing techniques; you get your pushing positions. And, let's not forget the childbirth film that, for some of you, shows more about having a baby than you ever wanted to see (thank you very much!). And as you're enduring this bizarre rite of passage, trying to absorb the information (without catching the eye of your husband or partner, because if you do, you'll both burst into uncontrollable laughter), you're feeling on some level as if it's bogus. Most of the time it *is* bogus because what you're doing is arming yourself with a random array of labor techniques that may or may not have anything to do with who you are and what comes naturally to you.

We've said it before. You don't change all of a sudden into an entirely different person in childbirth. You're *you*, having a baby, and what you'll be doing to cope with contractions depends entirely on your unique mix of temperament, personality, likes, dislikes, and desires. What works for you in your everyday life when you're stressed and in pain is what will work for you when you're in labor.

The following questions will help you match yourself up with what you already do and show you how that might look once you're in labor. It may be one of these strategies or a combination of them that helps you through. Remember, this list isn't all inclusive. *You* know what feels right. Going with what does feel right will get you through labor the best way you know how.

The Labor Coping Strategies Match

When you're in pain do you stay still or need to move around?
If you like to be *still*, curled up in bed or hunkered down on the couch, you'll most likely be doing the same thing in labor except you'll be in your hospital bed. You may have heard that being upright and walking during labor is a good thing because you're using gravity to help bring the baby down. That may work in theory, but if that's not what you feel like doing, then it's not necessarily a good thing for you. You're naturally someone who needs to be quiet to regroup.

If you find solace, comfort, and release through *motion*, you may be rocking in a rocking chair; sitting, swaying, or bouncing lightly on a birth ball; or standing and leaning over your raised bed, while you sway or do little knee bends. Depending on how far along you are in your labor, you may want to walk the hospital halls. There's most likely a well-worn path past the newborn nursery that can offer inspiration. What's key for you is to get the comfort or release that movement gives you without exhausting yourself. Once you're in active labor, even if you do like to move around, you might not feel at all like walking. That's OK. Moving around may not be right at every juncture of your labor.

When you're in pain, do you take pain relief immediately? Or, do you wait until the pain gets to be too much?
If you take it at the first sign of pain, you may be planning on getting an epidural as soon as you feel the least bit of discomfort. Keep in mind that some doctors want you to wait until you're in active labor, three to four centimeters dilated, before getting an epidural. Depending on how intense your contractions are, waiting may be possible, especially with the right support system and coping strategies. However, if you want the option of having an epidural sooner, make sure far in advance of the onset of labor, that you and your doctor have reached an understanding about this.

If you are the type who generally waits until you get to the point where you can't take the pain any longer before seeking relief, that's probably what you'll do in labor. Before you get to that point, you'll rely on whatever coping strategies are right for you.

Do you take a shower or bath to chill out?
If so, being in water may be a great place for you during labor because that's what helps you feel better. Spend as much time as you need laboring in the shower or, if your water hasn't broken, in the Jacuzzi—if your hospital has one. Just as a warm shower or soak helps you relax and let go in your everyday life, it can have the same effect on you in labor, providing some relief and helping you better relax with the contractions, which ultimately allows them to be more effective.

What kind of support do you need from your spouse or partner?
Whatever you normally like him to do to help you relax and get through a tough time is the kind of support you need. If hearing his voice helps quell your anxiety, it might be helpful for him to talk you through your contractions. For example, "You're at fifteen seconds; now you're at thirty; you're halfway; OK, the contraction's over." On the other hand, you may be the one who does all the talking and he reassures you periodically. "It's OK. You're doing great." If touch is part of the way he helps you cope or soothes you, massage might work. Perhaps you find it comforting when he does a certain thing such as tickling your arm or petting your hair. Or, maybe you don't like to be touched when you're uncomfortable but you need him to stay close by. You'll need different things from him at different points in your labor. If what he's doing isn't working, he can always move on to something else that will. Whatever systems the two of you already have in place are the ones to depend on in labor.

Do you use guided imagery, hypnosis, meditation, or yoga to relax?
If thinking about being on a beach in the Caribbean or focusing on your breathing or a mantra helps you calm your body and mind, then these strategies may very well work for you in labor. The deep relaxation that they produce allows you to let go so your labor can move forward. What won't work is thinking that you can all of a sudden learn to meditate or go into a hypnotic trance while you're in labor. Techniques like these only come naturally and easily if you've been doing them.

Are you a private person?
If privacy is important to you, think about hanging signs on the outside and inside of your closed door that say "Please Knock Gently" and "Please Close the Door Behind You." Safeguard your privacy by designating a buffer person who can shield you from people you're not comfortable with during labor. This buffer person could be your spouse or partner or someone else you trust who knows your sensi-

tivities. If you're modest, let your doctor or midwife know in advance what it is that might make you uncomfortable. Knowing that they have an understanding of what you are all about will reduce some of your anxiety and help you feel safe.

Are you outgoing and gregarious?

If you feel best when you're around people, then feedback and group support will probably be very important to you in labor. It may be that once you're in the thick of labor, you won't feel like talking, but you'll still need those people by your side, supporting you the way you need to be supported.

Are you sensitive to your surroundings?

The more "at home" you feel, the safer and more relaxed you'll be, giving your labor its best chance to progress. So make your hospital room your own. Get yourself cozy with your own pillows and comforter. Put familiar photos up on the walls. Put lavender oil on a washcloth to mask the hospital smell and encourage relaxation. Depending on what you prefer, pull down the shades and dim the lights or turn the lights up bright.

Do you like quiet, white noise, or music?

If you like quiet, shut your door to keep out the sounds of "paging Dr. Blah-Blah-Blah" and the rattling of the food service trays. Hang a sign on it that says something like "Please Knock Quietly and Shut Door Gently." Turn off the fetal monitor audio if you find it distracting. If you like to be cocooned in a blanket of white noise, bring a sound machine from home. Put the TV on low if background noise is comforting to you. Play music that helps you relax.

What About "The Breathing"?

We know for a fact that you've been breathing without any guidance from anyone for your entire life. We also know that whatever kind of breathing you naturally do under stressful circumstances is exactly what you'll do in labor. This may come as a shock to you, but you've already got this breathing business down. You're not going to "hee hee" and "hoo hoo" your way through contractions (unless those are the sounds that you normally make when you breathe). What you'll fall back on is what you do already.

> Whatever kind of breathing you naturally do under stressful circumstances is exactly what you'll do in labor.

Here's a simple way to reacquaint yourself with the way you breathe when you're feeling stress or pain:

1. Say the following to yourself: "I'm completely freaked out and I need to get centered" or "I'm really stressed and I need to get it together."
2. Then breathe.

Notice how you do it—whether you breathe in and out of your nose or just your mouth, whether you breathe through pursed lips or make a certain sound. Do you keep your eyes open or closed? Do you sway? Notice your rhythm as you try to settle yourself down. This is the breathing you'll do in labor when you say to yourself, "OK. That's not feeling so good. I need a little help to get through this contraction." You might find that you sigh deeply before you begin and after you're done (that's known as a cleansing breath in childbirth lingo). It doesn't matter how many breaths per minute, whether it's abdominal or diaphragmatic, or if flames flare from your nostrils. All that matters is that you breathe the way you naturally do. If you force yourself to breathe any other way, you'll eventually abandon it because it just doesn't work.

Once your labor picks up, so will your breathing. It will naturally move from the slow, methodical, "I'm just going to get it together" rhythm to your everyday rhythm. What does that look like on you? Just breathe normally (really!). If it's your habit to make a

---

■ Dr. Jekyll or Ms./Mrs. Hyde?

You've probably heard stories about women who've "lost it" during labor, and you may be wondering if (or even dreading that) it could happen to you because no matter what happens, how could it possibly be good? Here's the reality check. If you do happen to "lose it," it's not as if all of a sudden you snap and your spouse or partner stands by completely horrified as you transform into a woman possessed. He'll have seen you graduate to that place over a period of time and (surprise, surprise!) he'll be used to the way you "lose it" because he'll most likely have seen it before. Whether you cry, curse like a sailor, or speak sharply to him, you'll do what you normally do when the going gets tough. You may be working harder than you've ever worked to keep up with your labor, but you're still you. And here's some perspective—your "losing it" will not be a defining moment; it's just a small snapshot in the course of a whole experience. And letting go of your "social graces" is one way of knowing that your labor is progessing.

Your spouse or partner isn't going to all of a sudden become someone else either. What you see is what you get. So if you think you might need something that he can't provide, figure out in advance who else can. A spouse or partner who generally takes a background role won't all of a sudden become a leader. And if he's never even given you a back scratch, he's not going to become an expert at Swedish massage during your delivery. But, if he's always been the calm in the eye of your emotional storm, then that's how he'll help you weather your labor. Or, if he's the only one who can make you laugh when you're anxious or stressed out, he'll provide that comic relief that you've come to depend on so well.

---

sound when you're in pain (like ohhhh, ahhhh, ummmm, etc.), you might make that same sound when your contractions get intense. The sound gives you a place to let go and can act like a metronome to help you find your rhythm. Along with your breathing, you might do any movement or mannerisms that you usually do, such as flexing and pointing your feet, flicking your fingers, rocking, and so on.

"Formalized" Breathing

When you get to a point where your everyday breathing no longer helps, but you still *want* to use breathing to cope with the pain, it may be time for something fancier. For contractions that are particularly intense, you might try breathing in a pattern. For example, breathe two breaths with your typical sound and the third breath with a different sound, such as "Ahhh, ahhh, ohhhhh . . . ahhh, ahhh, ohhhhh" (substitute whatever sounds come naturally to you). Repeat your sequence through the contraction. This kind of breathing helps you get through each contraction by setting a goal, kind of like when runners say to themselves, "I just need to make it to that tree." ("*I* just need to get through two 'ahhhs' and an 'ohhhhh'.") Staying with your breathing pattern might be easier if someone breathes along with you. As always, if it works, great. If not, move on to whatever does.

What you do to make it through labor depends on this basic formula: you add the things that work for you and subtract the things that don't. You match yourself to the coping strategies that you naturally use when you're feeling stress and pain. Then if something's not working, you skip ahead to something else. It is all these little— and not so little—aspects about yourself that add up to the birth that's right for you.

· 9 ·

Medication:
Yes, No, Maybe So

Out of all the choices you have in childbirth, when it comes to deciding whether or not you'll want pain medication you're most likely to experience the evil eye of judgment. What's cast your way may be subtly implied or right in your face, but inevitably, it's a case of being damned if you do or damned if you don't. Maybe you're thinking that you *do* want pain medication. But when you ran that by your girlfriends, you just weren't prepared for comments like, "You're not fully experiencing childbirth" or "Those drugs aren't good for your baby." Maybe you're thinking that you *don't* want pain medication and you share that with your mother. You might hear, "Are you crazy? Why on earth would you choose to go through that kind of pain when you don't have to?" The same lack of support goes for what you might be reading in your childbirth books, in pregnancy magazines, or online. For every article and study that supports the way *you'd* like to give birth, you'll find just as many that don't. That's why we're here, to remind you of *the* most important consideration: *you* are having your baby. Your mother, your girlfriends, and all those "experts" are not.

What is important is finding what's right for you in labor and delivery and whatever it is you need to feel safe, cared for, relaxed, empowered, less anxious, less afraid, and so on. Only you can fill in the blanks. And your decision comes down to one consideration and one consideration only: whether using pain medication or not using pain medication will help you get through the experience in a way that works for you. In the end, the bottom line is that you feel good about what you did no matter what that looked like—whether you "om-ed" through contractions listening to a CD of Hindu chants, or you got your epidural five seconds after you arrived at the hospital, or you played it out as long as you could and then got pain medication in the home stretch. It's not about having the experience that other people want for you; it's about having the experience that you want for yourself.

> Your decision comes down to whether using pain medication or not using pain medication will help you get through the experience in a way that works for you.

To Medicate or Not to Medicate: How You'll Know

Right now you may be flip-flopping about whether you'll use medication or not. Maybe you're worried about how it will affect your baby, how it will make you feel, the possible side effects, how you'll know if you want it, when to get it, or when it's too late to get it. But just remember, as you deliberate about it now, you're not in the throes of labor. Once you are, you'll make your decision based on how your labor feels, both physically and emotionally. And usually when you're feeling like it's getting to be too much, you're not pondering things like how quickly the medication crosses the placental barrier or the size of the needle. All you're thinking is "I need to stop this pain now!" (And maybe you're quietly hoping that your anesthesiologist graduated at the top of his or her class.)

On the other hand, if your concern about medication or your commitment to having a drug-free birth takes precedence over your pain, you'll get through your labor by relying on whatever coping and alternative labor strategies work for you and help your labor progress. For example, you might try to stay home for as long as you can during early labor; have one-on-one professional coaching throughout your labor; move around however you need to; try different positions; shower or get in the tub (again, if your membranes are intact); breathe, moan, or yell through your contractions; meditate; listen to music; or be massaged. It might not be an "either/or" situation. You might find that what works best for you is a combination of nondrug strategies *and* pain medication.

> It's not about having the experience that other people want for you; it's about having the experience that you want for yourself.

It might be helpful to think of it this way: pain medication and nondrug coping strategies are different sides of the same coin—optimally they both accomplish the same thing. Instead of fighting your way through contractions, they allow you to let your labor do what it needs to do: dilate your cervix and push your baby out. And whether you do this through breathing, chanting, and/or having an epidural, you're helping your contractions do what they need to do.

Medications for Labor and Delivery

So here it is. Pain medication and epidural anesthesia are the two types of pain relief used in labor and delivery. Pain medication, usually narcotics, is given through your IV or by injection. It helps you relax—sometimes sleep—and takes the edge off your contractions. An epidural, which is given by an anesthesiologist, numbs your pain, taking most—if not all—of it away. Whichever you choose depends on what's happening with your labor and what you're trying to achieve. If you need to turn down your labor's decibel level in order to relax and better tap into your resources, pain medication can help you do that. If you need continuous pain relief for the rest of your labor, that's where an epidural can help.

> Pain medication and nondrug coping strategies are different sides of the same coin—optimally, they both accomplish the same thing. Instead of fighting your way through contractions, they allow you to let your labor do what it needs to do: dilate your cervix and push your baby out.

It's important to talk to your doctor or midwife about their practices regarding pain medication and epidurals way in advance of when you might need them. If this is your first baby, some practitioners might encourage you to wait to start an epidural until you're at least three to four centimeters dilated and in good, active labor (even though the research doesn't necessarily support this). Some won't give you pain medication or start an epidural (first-time mom or not) if you're very close to delivery. And then there are others who say the only time you *can't* have an epidural is after the baby has been born. That's why it's a really good idea to know these details in advance. Labor isn't the time to learn that what you want won't happen, given the way your doctor practices.

Pain Medications

Pain medications don't completely take the pain away. They reduce it enough to take the edge off, allowing you to relax and cope better with your contractions. If injected, they take about five to ten minutes to kick in. If given through your IV, they take effect almost immediately. You may feel like you've had a glass or two of wine. You may feel relaxed enough to nod off between contractions. They may make you nauseous, although many practitioners give pain medication in combination with a medication that counteracts nausea.

How do they affect your baby? They tend to make your baby sleepy, which isn't an issue when he or she is inside of you, but could be one if you deliver before the pain medication wears off. Although it's rare, a sleepy newborn might need some help breathing effectively. That's why practitioners avoid giving certain pain medication at the very end of your labor.

If you're someone who's worried or afraid that these kinds of drugs may make you feel too woozy or "out of it," consider starting with a half dose. You can always add more if you need to. And, just so you know, if you do have pain medication, you can still get an epidural.

Here are some questions to ask yourself during labor to decide if pain medication is what you need:

- Are you so tense, anxious, and/or exhausted that you're no longer able to cope with your contractions?
- Are you ready for some pain relief but not ready for, or even know if you want, an epidural?

If you answered yes to either of these questions, then pain medication might be right for you.

Epidural

An epidural is a continuous delivery of anesthetic that numbs the nerves to the uterus, cervix, and lower body so you no longer feel the pain of contractions, although later in labor you may feel pressure, which may mean it's time to push. Here's how it works. Those nerves are surrounded by spinal fluid and encased in a membrane called the dura. An epidural is an injection of medication *at* the dura but not puncturing it. A tiny flexible catheter is left in this space so that medication can be continuously delivered for pain relief. (A spinal, on the other hand, is an injection that punctures the dura and delivers medication directly into the spinal fluid. No catheter is left here. Spinal anesthesia only lasts a few hours. That's why it's really only used when short-term anesthesia is needed for procedures such as cesarean delivery and when an epidural catheter isn't already in place.)

Compared to epidurals of the past, anesthesiologists now have far more control over how much medication and what kind gets to those nerves. Optimally, their goal is to keep you pain-free without inhibiting your ability to move your legs. So instead of feeling completely numb from the waist down, you may be able to bend and stretch your legs and wiggle your toes. But that's based on the dose you're given and how you react to the medication. Depending on the kind of epidural you get, you might even be able to get out of bed and walk. (See the sidebar What's a Walking Epidural and Who's Actually Walking?)

Once you decide you want an epidural, who's allowed to stay in the room with you is up to hospital policy, your doctor, and the anesthesiologist. If it's important to you that your spouse or partner be there (and he can handle it and/or *wants* to be there), it's a good idea to get clearance for that from your anesthesiologist when he or she comes in to talk to you or ahead of time. If he is allowed to stay, he

▪ What's a Walking Epidural and Who's Actually Walking?

A walking epidural is an ultra-low-dose epidural containing two drugs: a narcotic and a local anesthetic. It's administered in stages via spinal injection and epidural catheter. First the narcotic is injected into your spinal canal and at that point your pain will lessen and you'll still be able to walk. Very little narcotic gets into your bloodstream or through to your baby. When you're ready for stronger pain relief, the anesthetic is given. You probably won't be capable of walking after that, but you should still be able to feel and move your legs (again, depending on the size of the dose you're given and how you react to the medication). Not all doctors or hospitals offer this kind of epidural, so if it's something you think you might want, find out in advance if it's an option.

is usually sitting nearby where he can't see what's going on behind you but can continue to be available to you emotionally.

Generally it's your nurse (and/or doula if you have one) who guides you through an epidural. She'll help you get into position—usually either curled up in bed on your side in a "C" or sitting on your bed so the anesthesiologist has access to your lower back. If you're uncomfortable once you're in position or you are having a contraction and want to move because you're uncomfortable, let your nurse and anesthesiologist know. There's usually some room for give-and-take while they're getting everything ready, although you will be asked to stay completely still for a couple of moments while they insert the catheter.

If you're feeling anxious, ask your anesthesiologist, nurse, or doula to talk you through each step along the way. Maybe you don't want to hear anything except that it's going well and it's almost over. Or, maybe you don't need any talking, just your music playing softly in the background. The same coping strategies that you've been rely-ing on in labor will help you through your epidural.

Here's how it generally goes. First you'll be given a local anes-thetic in your lower back. Then your anesthesiologist will slowly insert the epidural needle through which a very fine, flexible tube or catheter (about the diameter of a piece of angel hair pasta but much longer) is threaded. It could take some time (maybe up to fif-teen minutes) to find the right spot, insert the catheter through the needle, and take the needle out. During this part you might feel some pressure and even some twinges down your legs (kind of like those "zings" you might feel when you get Novocain). The catheter, which is then taped to your back, is connected to a pump that administers the epidural anesthetic. With help, you'll lie back down once everything's in place, and over the next fifteen to twenty min-utes you should start feeling more and more relief with each con-traction until, optimally, all you're feeling during a contraction is nothing or maybe some slight pressure. To push well, you generally need to feel some pressure. So discuss with your anesthesiologist beforehand that you'd like to be able to feel enough to push effectively.

Now it's time to really make use of the benefits of having bought time off from your labor. Rest up or sleep if you can. Do whatever you need to do to feel relaxed—dim the lights, listen to music, read or be read to, let the TV drone on in the background, or listen to others chatting quietly. Put a sign on your door that says "Sleeping, Please Enter Quietly." Regroup and recharge in whatever way works for you because eventually you're going to need to work again to push your baby out.

Sifting Through the Risks and Benefits

It's important to point out that how you feel about an epidural sit-ting here reading about it or learning about it in childbirth class could be very different from the way you might feel about it in the moment. For example, you might feel totally anxious about having one now, but when you're in labor you might be thinking "Just get me out of this." At that point, it may feel more like a benefit to you than a risk.

Or, if you're still crystal clear about whatever it is you don't like about an epidural, then you won't go there. Even though, in actuality, the serious risks are very small and side effects like a drop in blood pressure and itchiness can be easily managed, they could still feel very big to you. You'll rely on your own personal risk tolerance to make the decision that's right for you.

▪ Benefits and Risks of an Epidural

Benefits
- You usually have total pain relief.
- You're fully aware mentally.
- You can relax, rest, and/or sleep.
- Depending on the kind of epidural you get, you can move your lower body and sometimes stand or walk.
- If your labor has stalled because you're exhausted or fighting the pain and unable to relax, it may help you progress. (For example, your cervix hasn't budged from five centimeters for hours. Then you get an epidural and suddenly you're fully dilated.)

Risks and Side Effects
- Your blood pressure might drop, which in turn, could cause your baby's heart rate to drop. Both drops are usually reversed quickly with medication. (Some practitioners automatically give this medication to prevent any drop in blood pressure.) You'll also be given fluids through your IV before the epidural so your blood pressure has less of a chance of dropping.
- You may get really itchy. If it is making you crazy, you can g antihistamine for relief.

- Your labor might slow down enough that you need Pitocin in order to jump-start it again. (There are some situations in which an epidural can actually get labor moving, but there are other times when it can slow it down.)
- You might not be able to feel enough to push your baby out and need forceps or vacuum extraction. (See Chapter 11.)
- If you're a first-time mom and your epidural is started before three to four centimeters, some research suggests that your chances of having a cesarean delivery may be slightly increased if you are not in active labor.
- You may get a spinal headache if the dura (the membrane that surrounds the spinal cord) is mistakenly punctured. The procedure of patching the tiny hole by an injection of your own blood into the epidural space is really effective in getting rid of the headache.
- Occasionally, epidural anesthesia may partially numb the chest muscles you use for breathing. This may make you feel like you have a little weight on you or you may feel like there's an elephant sitting on your chest.
- Here's the one that freaks everybody out—temporary or permanent numbness, weakness, or paralysis in your lower body. And here's the reality check. Given how many thousands of women have epidural anesthesia, this risk is *extremely* rare. Statistically, you take far greater risk every day getting into your car.

If you're on the fence, here are some questions to ask yourself to help you figure out if an epidural is what you need:

- How long have you been in labor and are you exhausted?
- How depleted are your resources, both physically and emotionally?
- Have you come to the end of the line in terms of coping and need some time off to rest, sleep, or regroup?

- How close are you to being able to push? (The closer you are, the more likely you may be able to make it to the pushing stage without an epidural. Pushing *into* contractions can relieve a lot of the pain.)
- Are you making good progress in your labor?
- Do you have a professional labor support person helping you work with your contractions?

Keeping an Open Mind

When it comes to pain medication, you'll very likely go into labor with one of three mind-sets: (1) you'll know for sure that you want it, (2) you'll know for sure that you don't, or (3) you'll wait to see how you feel once you're there. Whatever mind-set you have, it's a decision that you may not be able to make with any semblance of certainty until you're actually experiencing labor. There's also the possibility that your labor may make the choice for you. It may turn out that what you want is at odds with what's actually happening in your labor.

> Whatever mind-set you have about medication, it's a decision that you may not be able to make with any semblance of certainty until you're actually experiencing labor.

For example, you may be adamant about getting an epidural as soon as you get to the hospital. But what if, once you get there, your doctor suggests that you should hold off for an hour or so to give your labor its best chance of progressing? What if you're so far along there just isn't time? You could have the epidural but it won't really take effect until after you've delivered.

Or, you may be just as adamant about *not* having any medication. But maybe you're overdue, your amniotic fluid levels are low, you need to be induced, and five hours of Pitocin have put you over your pain threshold. What if you've been laboring hard for twelve hours straight and you aren't dilating? Your midwife may feel that an epidural might give you the rest you need so you can relax and your cervix can dilate more effectively.

> *Dina: I'm not the type to take medicine even when I'm not pregnant. So it was a natural choice for me to sign on with a group of midwives with the plan to give birth without any pain medication. And then I went into labor. Back labor. The kind where not only were my contractions excruciating but the pain in the small of my back was still there even when the contraction was over. My midwife pulled every coping strategy known to mankind out of her bag—she had me on all fours; she tried warm compresses, cold packs, massage. After hours of trying different things, I got to the point where nothing helped. I was exhausted, and I hadn't even dilated past three centimeters. I needed to know my options. My midwife suggested that if I had an epidural I would be able to sleep and my cervix might move right along. While an epidural was never a real part of my plan, I knew I needed to stay flexible. And there was no way I was going to keep up with this for hours on end. I was just fighting to keep up with the pain and was not dilating.*

Dina went into labor with all the right stuff: clear aspirations and realistic expectations of herself. Except she didn't leave room for one very important thing—the unexpected, which in her case, was extremely painful back labor caused by her baby's position. Dina's midwife explained that if she continued not to dilate, there was a strong possibility that she could wind up having a cesarean delivery. She said that an epidural could give Dina some time off from the pain and give her cervix a chance to dilate. That advice, coupled with the near-constant pain she was feeling, helped Dina come to the realization that her antimedication stance wasn't really serving her.

Dina: Once the epidural kicked in, I had complete and utter relief. I think I fell asleep before the anesthesiologist left the room. After a few hours my midwife checked my progress and I had dilated to seven centimeters while I slept! I put out my arms, veins exposed, indicating that I wanted more medication, and half-joking said, "Wake me up when I'm back in my size six jeans." I went back to sleep and dilated to ten. And after about forty-five minutes of pushing, Sam was born. Meeting him for the first time was a wonderful, amazing experience, and I have absolutely no regrets about having an epidural. It was a real lesson for me about keeping an open mind.

While it's important to go into labor knowing what you want and need, it's just as important to go into it knowing that you won't know everything. There's really no predicting the kind of labor you'll wind up with. For Dina, the unexpected called for flexibility. And even though she wound up doing something that she never predicted she would, she felt strongly that if she hadn't, she would have been looking at a very different birth experience.

Going with Your Labor's Flow

The other possibility when it comes to the kind of labor you're dealt is that you may not have the choices you thought you would. You can go into labor armed with all the self-knowledge in the world and then not even get to apply it because your labor has different ideas.

Merrill: The afternoon before Annie was born I had been to my doctor, and I wasn't dilated at all. Then later that night, I started to feel a little uncomfortable. I took a hot shower and called my husband who was working late to tell him that I was feeling crampy and maybe he should come home. I really wasn't sure if it was labor or not because I wasn't in pain. After Robert came home my contractions became very intense and started coming fast. He went back downstairs to get a taxi to take us to

the hospital, and as soon as I sat down in the backseat my water broke
everywhere and I started feeling a lot of pain. I tried to do the breathing
I learned in childbirth class, but it was completely useless and I wound
up swearing like a truck driver through my contractions. When we pulled
up to the hospital, I barely made it out of the car. I couldn't believe it was
happening this way. Somehow we made it up to the delivery floor, and
I begged for the epidural that I had planned on getting throughout my
pregnancy. But I was almost fully dilated, and I was told there was no
time. My doctor never even made it to the hospital, and the resident, who
looked like she was about sixteen years old, ended up delivering Annie.
She was born less than an hour after we got to the hospital. Was I ecstatic
that I gave birth to a healthy baby girl? Of course I was. And although
I can laugh about it now and I know there wasn't anything I could have
done to change what happened, I wouldn't describe my labor experience
as anything I would have ever hoped for. And what's really crazy is that
everyone says how "lucky" I was to have such a short labor. They have
no clue.

You go into labor knowing what you know about yourself and
what you aspire to in your labor experience. And that's really the best
and the most you can know because labor is a story that unfolds in
a way that you won't be able to predict. While Merrill's experience
was fast and furious, first labors rarely happen this way. Merrill had
no choice but to be swept along in its currents. She didn't fight it or
lose herself in the process; she flowed with it (all the while swearing
up a storm!). Yes, she would have preferred to get relief from her
pain, but she knew that that was beyond her control.

Just the Way It Is

The most satisfying birth stories are born out of incorporating a kind
of flexible pragmatism into the way you approach labor and delivery. If you're feeling dead set against using pain medication or that

you'll absolutely die if you don't get it, troubleshoot your mind-set beforehand. Say for example, you know you don't want drugs. But what if you end up fighting your way through labor for hours and you're still not dilating? Would that be a circumstance where you'd be open to pain medication to try to avoid a cesarean? Or, say you know you want an epidural. But what if your labor moves really fast and there's just no time? Your flexible pragmatism might go into effect *after* your delivery, which didn't look anything like you thought it would.

> There are two plot lines in this story—what you want *and* what's happening with your labor. The most satisfying endings are the result of balancing the two.

Try to keep in mind that there are two plot lines in this story—what you want *and* what's happening with your labor. The most satisfying endings are the result of balancing the two. And if the balancing starts to feel like a tightwire act, cut yourself some slack. You've never done this before. It could take a little trial and error as well as some time to figure it out. You might talk through some contractions, laugh through some, and cry through others. Sometimes what you're doing will work up until a certain point and then you'll need to move on to something else. It works really well when you are flexible enough that you can adjust your coping strategies according to how you're feeling and how your labor is moving.

· 10 ·

When Labor Doesn't Go According to *Your* Plan

You may think you've got it all worked out. Your bags are packed. Your highlights look stunning. Your freezer is brimming with casseroles, lasagnas, and soups. Your favorite take-out places are on speed dial. Family and friends are at the ready. Your due date comes. And then it goes. Before you know it, the birth script that you've been writing in your head all these months evaporates into thin air.

Here's the point about labor. As hard as you might try, you just can't plan it. The only schedule that labor follows is its own. Unless you've already got an induction planned or a cesarean delivery scheduled, there's just no knowing when labor will arrive or, once it does, what it will look like. And, there's also this other person involved—your baby. Not only is it about what's right for you, it's also about what's right for her or him.

Delays and Road Blocks

Here are the possible itinerary deviations when it comes to labor: you could go a week or two past your original due date (that's the average length a practitioner is typically comfortable letting you go before an induction); your membranes could rupture but contractions don't start; you could have great contractions, but you're not dilating; your contractions may not be strong or regular enough to dilate your cervix; or your baby could be breech, meaning feet or bottom first, or transverse, meaning sideways (forget the silver spoon, how about a compass!).

When things aren't going the way you thought or hoped they would go, as frustrated, impatient, or disappointed as you might feel, you can still work with these deviations in a way that's in sync with what's right for you. Keep in mind that you're not completely at the whim of your labor. There are some things your doctor or midwife can do, *and* there are some things you can do when your labor doesn't go according to plan.

What You Can Do When Your Due Date Passes You Right By

The following options, depending on your belief systems, either can feel right up your alley or pretty ridiculous. Although most of them have been around forever and many people consider them tried-and-true methods for getting labor started or jump-started after stalling out, there have been very few scientific studies done to prove whether they work or not. But, for example, if having an induction is not part of your birth script and you're willing to try anything to avoid one, you might feel it's worth giving these alternatives a try.

> When things aren't going the way you thought or hoped they would go, as frustrated, impatient, or disappointed as you might feel, you can still work with these deviations in a way that's in sync with what's right for you.

Whatever you do, always do it with the approval of your doctor or midwife, some of whom may have very definite opinions regarding these labor starters and whether or not they're safe or you'd be a candidate. Assuming there are no problems with your pregnancy, he or she will want to check your cervix to see if it's inducible or if you're already dilated and that your baby is in a head-down position. If you get your practitioner's go-ahead, always use these approaches under the guidance of someone who is highly knowledgeable, which may be your midwife, physician, doula, acupuncturist, chiropractor, homeopath, or herbalist.

> Every day you wait, your odds of going into labor increase dramatically.

If You're Overdue and Trying to Avoid an Induction

- **Wait.** Contrary to what you might think, something *is* happening even though it may seem like nothing's going on. Every day you wait, your odds of going into labor increase dramatically. It all depends on whether you feel pressed for time because you're trying to avoid an induction or you have some room to gamble.
- **Sex.** OK, maybe you haven't stopped. Or, maybe sex is the last thing you're thinking about. But whether you're in the mood or not, semen is loaded with prostaglandins that can soften your cervix *and* orgasm can bring on contractions. Note: sex is *not* an option if your water has broken.
- **Nipple Stimulation.** You can do it by hand or with a breast pump. It helps your body produce oxytocin, which causes your uterus to contract.
- **Evening Primrose Oil.** Your body converts it to prostaglandin, which is the hormone-like substance that softens your cervix and can cause contractions. Evening primrose oil

comes in a gel-filled capsule that you can open and apply to your cervix. If the gel alone doesn't cause any crampiness or contractions, the next step might be to have your husband or partner put some gel on himself (that would be his penis) before you have sex. This gets you a double dose of prostaglandin through his semen and the evening primrose oil. Are you still with us? Good. Because it only gets better.

- **Castor Oil.** This labor starter has been used for generations. Very simply put, it can cause diarrhea and/or vomiting (oh yeah, that's pleasurable), both of which can bring on labor. But because it can cause dehydration and taking the proper dose (which is very small) is very important, only take it under the supervision of your practitioner.
- **Enema.** This works on the same principle as castor oil. The flushing out of your bowels can stimulate your uterus to contract.
- **Acupressure and Acupuncture.** Both are methods used by certified acupuncturists for stimulating uterine contractions. One of the most common acupressure points to stimulate contractions is the webbing between your thumb and pointer finger. You can apply pressure to this acupressure point yourself during labor in the hospital if you need to.
- **Herbs.** Certain herbs such as blue and black cohosh are said to ripen the cervix and bring on contractions. But they should only be used either under the direction of your practitioner or someone else who is highly knowledgeable about them (like an herbalist, naturopath, acupuncturist, chiropractor, or doula) *and* with your practitioner's go-ahead.

Getting a Derailed Labor Back on Track
- **If your membranes rupture but contractions don't begin.** Every option on the list above for overdue pregnancies is fair game here, too, *except* for intercourse or applying evening primrose oil to your cervix. Remember, if your membranes

rupture, you need to let your practitioner know. He or she will usually want labor to start within twelve to twenty-four hours because the risk for infection increases over time. Because of that, many doctors will recommend an induction if your water breaks and you have no contractions. But, if you'd like to wait for as long as you can to see if contractions start on their own, there should be room for discussion. (Note: between thirty-six to thirty-eight weeks you'll be tested to see if you carry the bacteria Group B streptococcus. If you test positive and your water breaks, you'll be started on IV antibiotics as soon as possible at the hospital and you may not have that twelve- to twenty-four-hour window.)

- **If you have contractions but they're not strong or regular.** You can wait it out, the thought being that they'll get stronger and/or more regular over time; you can have sex if your water hasn't broken; or you can try nipple stimulation and/or an enema. If you've had contractions for a while and you haven't been able to get any sleep, your practitioner may prescribe sleep medication.

When Your Baby Doesn't Read the Map

What do you do if your baby is breech? During most of your pregnancy it's fine for your baby to be in any position it wants. But if your baby is breech in the last month of pregnancy, it may stay breech, since there is a lot less room for it to flip. The following are options after you reach thirty-six weeks. But, at the same time, you should be discussing the option of external version (manually rotating your baby from the outside) with your doctor or midwife, a procedure only he or she can perform (see If Your Baby Is Breech).

- **Moxibustion.** A traditional Chinese medicine technique, moxibustion is usually done by an acupuncturist. In moxibustion, a stick or small incenselike cone of the dried herb moxa, or mugwort, is burned at an acupuncture point just above your pinky toe. Or, the tip of an acupuncture needle that has been inserted into the acupuncture point is wrapped in moxa and ignited. The burning of the herb is said to increase blood flow to the pelvic area and uterus and stimulate *qi* (Chinese for "life energy"), which causes the baby to turn. Although it may feel to you like some strange rite, the *Journal of the American Medical Association* gives it its stamp of approval, calling it a safe and effective method for turning breech babies. Only licensed acupuncturists can perform moxibustion. If you don't presently see an acupuncturist or know someone who does, your state acupuncture association or licensing board will have names of practitioners in your area.

- **Reverse gravity.** Some midwives suggest lying with stacked pillows under your hips for a set amount of time each day, the thought being that reversing the baby's gravity might encourage the baby to flip.

Labor Starters or Conversation Enders?

Choosing how to try to get labor going on your own is completely up to which methods feel right and which are just too freaky, or whether or not you even feel comfortable tinkering with nontraditional methods. You may just believe "it's not nice to fool with Mother Nature." Or, you may feel like giving Mother Nature a helping hand.

What to choose? If you're the type who does everything possible to avoid vomiting, then castor oil won't be at the top of your list. If you're needle phobic, then acupuncture isn't going to work for you either. And an enema? We'll leave that one up to you. You'll know what feels right. And if you're ready (already!) to get your labor going, you'll go for it.

Gwen: My first was born by cesarean because she was breech and they couldn't turn her. My second was the vaginal birth I didn't get with my first, so it wound up being a very healing thing for me. And my third I was planning to have with a midwife. I figured it was my last hurrah, and I wanted the experience to be as nurturing and intervention-free as I could get. Then my due date came and went, which was really surprising, since this was my third baby. And then I was in for an even bigger surprise. Because of my prior cesarean delivery and the risk of uterine rupture, I wouldn't be allowed to have an induction. If I went much more past my due date, my midwife would rupture my membranes to try to get my labor going. And if that didn't work, I would be face-to-face with a repeat cesarean. There was just no way I was doing that again without really needing one.

You may just believe "it's not nice to fool with Mother Nature." Or, you may feel like giving Mother Nature a helping hand.

The possibility of having her baby by cesarean, having already had a VBAC (vaginal birth after cesarean), made Gwen crazy. This baby would probably be her last and the thought of ending up with what she felt would be an unnecessary cesarean by default was really disturbing. It now became a race against time.

Gwen: With no contractions on the horizon, you name it, I tried it. With two young children running around and in the ninth month of pregnancy with my third, I wasn't exactly feeling like a sex goddess, but that's what my doula suggested (for which my husband will be eternally grateful). Sex didn't push me into complete contractions, so I added more fuel to the fire. I tried some herbs, I had some acupuncture, and my massage therapist worked on a lot of the trigger points for labor. But I have a suspicion that it was my breast pump that did it. Every time I used it, I got strong contractions. And then the floodgates opened, it seemed, when my water broke. Given that I had trouble getting my labor started, now there was no stopping it. I got to the hospital at 11:30 P.M. and my daughter was born at 12:46 A.M.

Looking back on the whole experience, Gwen wondered how much her head had played into her being overdue. Even though she was in love with the idea of a third baby, there was something else going on for her. She knew that with a new baby on the scene, the balanced family life that she and her husband had worked so hard to create was about to be disrupted. What it was that finally triggered Gwen's labor, she'll never really know for sure. Whether it was being backed up against an unwanted cesarean, trying to get labor going on her own, or resolving her feelings about having a third child—something shifted and Gwen wound up with the birth experience she had hoped for.

What Your Doctor or Midwife Can Do

Doctors and midwives have a set number of cards that they can play either to get labor going or restart one that's stalled. They may even be able to turn your breech baby. These options are sometimes limited by hospital policy and/or driven by individual styles of practice. Which card is played and, in what order, will vary from practitioner to practitioner.

If You Go Past Your Due Date

Once you go past your due date, your doctor or midwife will start talking about an induction. How long you can wait varies, but many practitioners don't feel comfortable with you going beyond seven to ten days. Now, even though it wasn't part of your "plan," being induced may suit you just fine. Maybe you've had your fill of being pregnant and you're ready to meet your baby. Having an induction means you'll no longer be in limbo, wondering when you're going to go into labor. Or, maybe having an induction never even crossed your mind and you're feeling really disappointed at the possibility.

How an Induction Is Done

It may be as simple as a really vigorous internal exam at your prenatal visit. This isn't fun but it can often nudge labor into action. Another relatively simple strategy is to "strip your membranes." If your cervix is soft enough, your practitioner will run his or her finger over the area between your cervix and amniotic sack to release prostaglandin in the hope that it will stimulate contractions.

An induction in the hospital can be done in or out of your bed. For example, you could be sitting on your birth ball or in a rocking chair. And you can still use most of your same coping strategies, except for the shower or the tub because you'll be attached to the fetal monitor. If your cervix is not yet ready, your practitioner may start by putting a synthetic prostaglandin (either a tablet, wafer, or gel) into your vagina to help ripen (soften, thin out, and slightly dilate) your cervix. After about two hours of monitoring, you may be able to move and walk around freely. In addition to or instead of the prostaglandin, you may be given Pitocin, the synthetic form of oxytocin, through an IV to get your contractions going. You'll start with a small dose, which will be increased intermittently, trying to simulate labor. If you don't have an epidural and your contractions are feeling too intense, you can work with your doctor or midwife to tailor the dose so you can manage the induction better.

At some point during your induction your doctor or midwife may also suggest rupturing your membranes (your baby's head needs to be low enough to avoid the complication of cord prolapse, which is when the umbilical cord comes down before the baby). The hope is that rupturing your membranes allows the baby to move down and apply its head to your cervix to help it dilate with each contraction. This, coupled with Pitocin, may make your contractions that much more effective.

Rupturing membranes sounds terrible, but it really doesn't hurt because the amniotic sac has no nerve endings. The truth is it's more like poking a small hole in the sac to create a leak. Your practitioner uses something that looks like a long-handled crochet hook (without the hook part), which they insert through your vagina and cervix.

When an Induction Is Part of Your Plan

Sometimes one person's idea of a labor gone offtrack may actually be another person's labor plan. Maybe you've decided an induction is what you want because of your spouse's or partner's work schedule or your children's school schedule. Or, perhaps you really want a certain doctor or midwife to be at your birth. You may actually *choose* to choreograph your delivery.

Rita: It was five days before my due date and we were careening toward Christmas. I was getting more and more anxious because: A. I didn't want my baby to have to share his birthday with Christmas; B. My entire family was coming in from all over; and, most important, C. My husband had to travel for a job interview the week between Christmas and New Year's. We were both really worried that I would go into labor when he was out of town. At my prenatal visit that day I only half-jokingly suggested to my doctor that it would be really convenient if this baby came next Tuesday—before Christmas, before my husband's trip, and while my family was in town to help out. I was shocked when my doctor said, "Let's see if that could be a possibility." He checked my cervix and said it was favorable. We came up with a plan. If I didn't go into labor over the weekend on my own, I would come back to the office on Monday to be checked. And given that the baby and I were both fine, we'd go ahead with an induction on Monday night.

Even though Rita was trying hard to keep it together and let her labor take its own course, the stress that she and her husband, Louis, were feeling because of the "not knowing" was really taking its toll. When they realized that having an induction might very well be an option and would guarantee that Louis would be there for the birth of their baby, a huge weight was lifted off their shoulders.

> Sometimes one person's idea of a labor gone offtrack may actually be another person's labor plan.

Rita: I was admitted to the hospital on Monday night. They put prostaglandin gel on my cervix, and I got something to help me sleep. My doctor came in to check me early Tuesday morning and they started the Pitocin. I was a little worried about how I would handle the contractions, so I asked if they would increase the dose slowly. I did OK through the morning—I was in bed and in the rocker—but by early afternoon I was ready for an epidural. I slept some and was ready to push later that night. Louis was with me every step of the way, and our baby was born shortly after midnight. Although having a scheduled induction was never part of our plan, we're both so grateful that we didn't have to leave it up to chance. I couldn't imagine not having my husband by my side or that he wouldn't be there for the birth of our son.

A planned induction isn't for everyone. Along with the peace of mind that can come from knowing when your baby will be born also come risks if this is your first baby—risks such as a potentially long labor and an increased chance of needing a cesarean, especially if your cervix is not ready. For first-time moms, many doctors will recommend that you hold off on an induction either altogether or until it's absolutely necessary. But for Rita and Louis, the risk that he might not be there for the birth of their baby outweighed the others. With the help of their doctor, they were able to come to the right decision for them.

If you already have a scheduled induction or cesarean delivery on the calendar, or if you're considering one, you're bound to run up against other people's opinions about it. There's plenty being said about the pros and cons of scheduling your birth. But the true litmus test for making this decision comes down to one thing and one thing only: whether or not it feels right for you. You'll get to your answer based on how you've been making decisions your entire life. Whether that means researching it from top to bottom with a fine-tooth comb, talking it through with your practitioner, weighing the risks and the benefits, and/or just going with your gut.

If Your Membranes Rupture but Contractions Don't Start

If you're one of the few whose membranes rupture but hours go by with no contractions, most doctors or midwives will begin an induction, although some might first suggest alternative methods such as nipple stimulation.

If You Have Contractions but You're Not Dilating

If you have contractions but they're not frequent or long enough to dilate your cervix, your doctor or midwife might suggest rupturing your membranes if they're still intact (and if your baby's head is low enough to avoid cord prolapse).Your practitioner may also want to start Pitocin. The hope is that rupturing your membranes and/or starting Pitocin at a low dose and increasing it gradually will make your contractions more effective and you'll dilate.

If an epidural isn't part of your plan but you've been laboring for hours trying different labor strategies, you're not dilating, and you're headed for a cesarean delivery, ask yourself: "Is there anything else I'd like to try or need to do, so no matter what happens, I won't wonder at the other end, 'What would have happened if . . . ?'" And does that include considering an epidural (which you would get anyway in the event of a cesarean)? An epidural isn't necessarily right for everyone, but in this case it might help you relax or sleep so your cervix can dilate and you could deliver vaginally. We call it our "Leave No Stone Unturned" Theory. This way, after your birth, you're not beating yourself up by asking yourself afterward, "Would I have avoided a cesarean delivery if only I'd had an epidural?"

If Your Baby Is "Posterior"

Occiput posterior means your baby is "sunny-side up"—he or she is facing your belly rather than facing your back. Most babies will rotate to a face-down position during labor, but it usually takes time, and, in the meantime, you might be slow to dilate, contractions could be irregular, and you could have some pretty intense back pain. If you have an epidural, your support team may actually flip you gently from side to side to try to get your baby to rotate. If you don't have an epidural, your doctor, midwife, nurse, or doula may suggest laboring on all fours or other positions to take the weight of the baby's head off your back and use gravity to get your baby to turn. They might also suggest rolling back and forth or side to side on a birth ball, or swaying your hips back and forth while standing or on all fours in the bed, in order to turn your baby. Your doctor or midwife might eventually suggest an epidural and possibly Pitocin to

---

■ **The Intervention Equation**

True or False? Once you start Pitocin you're on a roller-coaster ride to a cesarean because rupturing your membranes + Pitocin + an epidural = guaranteed cesarean delivery.

False: The fact of the matter is, if labor isn't progressing on its own and Pitocin is given to promote contractions, Pitocin actually *decreases* your risk of having a cesarean delivery.

---

boost your contractions in order to get your baby's head to rotate. If you're still not dilating, your contractions are stalling, and it looks like you're headed for a cesarean delivery, remember the "Leave No Stone Unturned" Theory and consider which strategies you will want to have used so you emerge confident at the other end about what you did do or decided not to do.

Chances are good that you've been warned that the more interventions you have in your labor the more you increase your chances for needing a cesarean. While that's true in general, it's not always so clear-cut whether it's the interventions that increase your risk or the reasons behind *why* you needed them in the first place. In some cases, interventions can actually *decrease* your chances of having a cesarean delivery. If you're not dilating, having your membranes ruptured and getting Pitocin to bring on or strengthen contractions may actually help you avoid one.

The downside of going into your labor with the mind-set of avoiding every intervention no matter what is that you are left with fewer options and less opportunity to work with your labor when it doesn't go according to plan. Keep going back to what's really important to you. Is it avoiding every intervention or is it avoiding a cesarean? And remember, one doesn't necessarily lead to the other.

If Your Baby Is Breech

By thirty-six weeks most practitioners are looking to see that your baby has settled head-down into your pelvis. If that's not the case, it isn't to say that your baby can't turn at any time, but the chances are less likely because now there's only so much room left in there (as you well know). Many practitioners are trained to do a procedure called an *external version* during which they turn your baby from the outside of your belly to shift him or her into a head-down position. If you're a candidate, there's more than a 50 to 60 percent chance that it will work, although some babies have been known to flip right back into their original breech position. To minimize your baby's window of opportunity for that, your doctor may wait to do an external version until you're at thirty-seven or thirty-eight weeks.

External versions are done in the hospital. Your practitioner may give you medication to relax your uterus. He or she then applies persistent, firm pressure to your baby's head and bottom over a period of one to three minutes to gradually get him or her to rotate. It can be uncomfortable, but the baby gets moved in stages so you have moments in between to regroup.

One risk of an external version is that your baby's heart rate might drop. It usually climbs back up to normal pretty quickly. You and your baby will be monitored before and after the procedure to make sure you're both fine. If your baby can't be turned, most likely you'll be scheduled for a cesarean delivery.

Sometimes a breech isn't discovered until you're actually in labor (medicine is not a perfect science; sometimes a baby's behind feels like a head). There are some practitioners who will attempt a version in early labor, but only if your membranes are intact.

Amanda: My husband and I were in the car on our way to meet some friends for dinner when my water broke. I figured I'd call my doctor to let her know and then we'd head back home to wait for contractions to start. My doctor was fine with that but she wanted me to come into the hospital to do a quick check on the baby, since it was now 7 P.M. and I probably wouldn't be admitted until sometime the next morning. When we got to the hospital and she examined me, she discovered that what should have been a head down below was really my baby's bottom. An ultrasound confirmed it. My baby was breech.

Amanda went into the hospital for what she thought would be a routine check and it turned into something completely unexpected. Instead of going home to wait for her contractions to start as she had planned, she was heading for the operating room.

Amanda: I was pretty shell-shocked as I was being prepped for surgery. A version wasn't possible because my water had broken. I couldn't quite get my head around the idea that this was the way it was going for me. I knew that the good news was that I was just a few hours away from holding my baby in my arms. All I could think about was what would have happened if my doctor hadn't had me come in for that quick check. I would have labored all night long and then come into the hospital to find out that my baby was breech. That would have been beyond disappointing—all that work and then a cesarean? Although I did feel cheated out of the birth that I thought I'd have, I would have felt far more cheated if that had happened.

Amanda had approached childbirth from the very beginning with a wait-and-see attitude. She wanted to try to have her baby without pain medication if it worked out that way, but she was flexible about having an epidural if it didn't. It was this frame of mind that got her through her cesarean delivery. Yes, she was shocked that she ended up in surgery and she felt sad that she wasn't going to have her baby vaginally. But because her approach included leaving room for the unexpected, she didn't end up feeling resentful or that anything was done without her understanding why.

The Best-Laid Plans

It's human nature to head into labor and delivery wanting everything to be whatever your expectations of "perfect" may be. Then reality pays you a visit and you're a week late with no signs that your baby's budging and you are so done with lugging your watermelon of a belly around all day. Or, your baby is feetfirst and not flipping, and the birth you thought you'd have has turned on its head (or not, in your case). Or, you might be grappling with when it would be better for you and your family for this baby to be born versus leaving it up to fate.

You're at a place in your story where your expectations are out of sync with what's actually happening for you and that's a tough spot to be in. Whatever you're feeling is completely valid, so go easy on yourself. Try not to make yourself feel worse by judging your feelings or the circumstances. Instead, take a look at what you need for you in that moment. That's what can help you feel like you have some control, especially when you're spinning out of it.

When things aren't going the way you had hoped they would, you do have a menu of options that you can consider, as does your doctor or midwife. You may choose to do something or you may choose to do nothing. But knowing that at least you have some choice in the matter can help you feel like you have some control. Even if it turns out that what you choose doesn't impact the outcome, you can feel satisfied and more confident that you did what you could. You struck a balance between doing what you need to do for yourself to feel better *and* going with the flow.

· 11 ·

Giving Birth: "Fully"

You're nearing the end of your labor story. You've been measuring it out in centimeters, and now you're almost to the point where you're fully dilated and ready to start pushing your baby out. If you had an epidural, you might be sleeping your way through those last few centimeters. If you haven't, your contractions are probably feeling pretty intense and you're relying on whatever coping strategies work for you to see you through. You could very well be feeling like you've had it. You want out of here. Let somebody *else* have this baby. Usually by the time it feels like you've reached the end of the line, it's a signal that you're pretty close to pushing.

This part of labor is called *transition*. It literally is the transition between the last bit of dilation and the start of pushing. In order to dilate those last remaining centimeters, your contractions may need to pick up speed or strength, or sometimes both. It's sort of like sprinting at the end of a long race. The signs that herald transition can be both emotional and physical. You might feel irritable and be able to give only one-word answers because you're so consumed by your contractions. As your body shifts gears in response to all the work it's doing, you might also feel nauseous. You might start shaking or shivering uncontrollably even though you're not cold. You may feel scared and overwhelmed, thinking something's not right. But what's happening is completely normal.

Even though babies are born every day, labor is a powerful experience. The fact that you can grow another human being in your body and then push it out is extraordinary. Your body can't help but react dramatically to what it's doing and what it's about to do. Some of these transition signs could take you by surprise. You might not understand what's happening to you and feel frightened by that. Not to worry. Your body is doing exactly what it's supposed to be doing.

Support During Transition

When the sensations and emotions of labor are at the point where they're coming as intensely as they might in transition, you may not have the capacity or the wherewithal to let your support team know what's going on for you. *You* might not even know what's going on for you. But a good support team will; they'll offer you the feedback, encouragement, and reassurance that you may need.

> Having someone you can really lean on during the hard parts of your labor can make all the difference in the world.

Heather: Throughout the last few months of my pregnancy I prepared for labor and delivery kind of like the way I imagine people prepare for a marathon—getting familiar with the terrain during all the different stages. I read about what early labor would be like. I knew from there I'd move into active labor and the turning point would be transition. I figured if I had an idea where I was headed each step of the way and what I'd be feeling, I'd be better able to handle it. I got to the hospital in the thick of labor and was able to cope for a while. But even with all the reading I had done beforehand, I wasn't really ready for transition. It was so intense and it took everything I had just to keep up. I'd finish one contraction and another would start right away. I was panicking. And somehow my doula just knew. When I started to feel like "Oh my God, here comes another one?!!," she locked eyes with me and said, "You're almost done with dilating and very soon you're going to push. Just stay right with me."

For Heather, it was as if someone had reached out a hand to her during a time when she felt like she was drowning. She sank into her doula's eyes and the breathing that they did together worked like a life raft. That, along with her doula's reassuring words, kept her afloat through transition.

Heather: I found out later that, although it seemed like an eternity, we breathed together for only about five or six contractions. And then in the midst of this trancelike haze, suddenly I felt like I had to go to the bathroom and I thought, "Maybe that means I'm ready to push." And I remember my doula saying, "Let's get the doctor to see if your baby's ready." With the next contraction, I felt more pressure and my doctor said I could start pushing. It took some time to get the hang of it and move my baby down, but I felt a lot less pain because now I was pushing into my contractions. Even still, it was exhausting. Finally, about two and a half hours later, my seven-pound, eight-ounce baby boy was born. When I look back on my birth, I remember transition as the place where I thought I just couldn't do it anymore. But because there was someone there who knew what I was going through and knew exactly what to do and say, I got through it.

Having someone you can really lean on during the hard parts of your labor can make all the difference in the world. Throughout most of Heather's labor, that person was her husband. But during transition, her doula was the anchor she needed when her labor became bigger than she ever thought it would. And that's just how a good support team works. Depending on their roles, each member steps up to the plate right when they're needed.

Signs That You're Getting Ready to Push

So how *will* you know when it's almost time to start pushing? Whether you realize it or not, everyone in the room will be secretly focusing on one thing: your rectum. If you have an epidural, they're patiently waiting for you to start talking about pressure. If you don't, they're patiently waiting for you to start talking about having to go to the bathroom (or trying to scramble out of bed in an absolute panic so you can). If you do happen to feel that unmistakable urge, you might be convinced (and appalled) that you're about to go right then and there. But you can stop panicking. What you're actually feeling is the result of your baby moving down and pressing on your rectum. The pressure you feel may even cause you to involuntarily start pushing during a contraction. But no matter what degree of pressure you feel, it's a sure sign that you're that much closer to meeting your baby.

> The fact that you can grow another human being in your body and then push it out is extraordinary.

Although having rectal pressure can be helpful because it gives you a sensation to push into, it's not required. You might never feel that "infamous" urge to push, depending on your anatomy, the size of your baby, or whether you've had an epidural. No, you haven't failed Labor 101. You're just as capable of pushing your baby out whether you feel rectal pressure or not.

Once You Get the Green Light

Some practitioners will give you the go-ahead to start pushing as soon as you're fully dilated. Others might wait a little while longer until your baby has started to make its way down, letting that urge or pressure build so you can use it as a guide to push into. Regardless of when you start, here's the lowdown on pushing: it might take some time to get the hang of it. It's pretty common at the beginning to feel like you're not pushing "right," particularly if you've had an epidural, because you might not be able to fully feel what you're doing. This is when the term "coaching" really takes on its literal meaning, because that's what your doctor, midwife, nurse, doula, and/or partner/spouse are doing. Your support team guides you to push effectively, and when it's not effective, they help you adjust it.

How to Push

As long as your uterus is contracting, you want to capitalize on that and push along with it. Here's generally how pushing goes. As a contraction begins to build, you might take a couple of breaths. And then at the height of that contraction, you may be instructed to hold your breath and push to the count of eight. Then you'll exhale, quickly refill your lungs, hold your breath, and push again for eight counts. You'll probably do this one more time. You usually get about three good pushes per contraction. Once your contraction is over, you regain your natural breathing and your team can give you ice chips, wipe you with a cool washcloth, and give you the support you need while you rest up for the next contraction.

Instead of pushing in this more formalized way, you may be left to push whenever you feel the urge. Do what comes naturally: grunting, groaning, moaning, yelling, or singing your baby down and out. Or maybe you don't make any sound at all. And if you need to make any adjustments in order to push more effectively, you'll be coached through them. No matter how you push, it's essential to feel completely trusting of those around you to do whatever it is you need to do to get your baby out.

When Push Comes to Shove

Every childbirth method has its own ideas around the breathing, breath-holding, and pushing combination, as does every doctor or midwife. But all that really matters is what feels right to you *and* what's effective. Maybe that "standard" combination, described above, works perfectly for you. Then, go for it. Maybe it's uncomfortable for you to hold your breath for eight counts (you might feel as if you're about to push your eyeballs out instead of your baby). Then try holding your breath for only six counts and see if that works better for you. Maybe after a while your third push starts to peter out because you're tired. So cut back to two pushes for the next few contractions (we promise we won't tell the pushing police).

It's pretty common to feel intimidated as you try to get your system of pushing down. It may take a bit to coordinate it all. Give yourself a break. And some time. You'll get it. If you start to feel as if you're being coached by a drill sergeant and you're worried that you're going to have to do push-ups soon because you're not getting it right, say something. Be assured, nobody's judging you—but it could feel like they're "yelling" at you. That's because everyone in the room is hyperfocused on helping you push as best you can. You'll feel really supported and work best when the energy in the room matches what you need. That could range from lots of cheering and rah-rah to quietly whispered encouragement. It all depends on you.

Here's the Poop on Pushing

We'd like to offer a little advice that may be helpful to you regarding pushing. (And it's the last time we'll talk about anything that has to do with pooping. We promise!) Pushing out a baby is pretty much like pushing out a bowel movement. Not particularly profound, but true. And (what a relief) you don't need to learn this in childbirth class! You do this kind of pushing every day (or so) of your life, although granted, not in this capacity.

And here's the last word about pooping. Sometimes the biggest obstacle to pushing effectively is the fear of pushing out a bowel movement in the process. We completely get it. But you've got to know it's nothing new to the hospital staff. And everybody in that room respects you and the amazing work you're doing. If you feel like you're fixating on your fear and it's hindering your progress, just keep re-focusing on what is really the most important thing: getting your baby out.

Pushing Positions

Just like you've been laboring in a way that works for you, the same goes for the way you push your baby out. You can't control how long it takes, but you can make sure that you're doing it in a way that feels right and is working. That could mean lying propped up in bed or on your side, kneeling on all fours, or standing. You may have heard that squatting is the most effective pushing position because it makes use of gravity to help bring your baby down and out. So if it feels natural to you, then great. If it doesn't, then move on to something else. You may need to try a few different positions before you find what's most comfortable *and* effective.

> *Keisha: I felt best lying on my side and that's where I started out push-ing. My nurse helped me get into a tuck with one knee to my chest and I pushed like that for a while. But they could tell that my baby wasn't rotating so I tried a bunch more positions—at least four or five. I was on all fours, on my knees with my head down on the bed in my hands, and squatting while my husband held me. But no matter what I tried, my baby wasn't coming down. I was wiped out and ready to give up. Then my nurse suggested I lie flat on my back for a couple of contrac-*

tions because maybe my baby couldn't get under my pubic bone. I remember thinking that was crazy. Everything that I had read talked about gravity—"whatever you do, don't lie flat!" But my nurse explained that by lying flat I might be able to give my baby a little more room between my pubic bone and my lower back to do the limbo under my pubic bone. That was all my baby needed. After about five good pushes he came out crying. And as they put him in my arms, my husband and I were so overcome with happiness and relief, we cried, too.

Where Your Spouse or Partner Will Be

Remember, you and your spouse or partner are in this together. And where he is physically while you're pushing depends on what you need *and* where he feels he needs to be. Some spouses naturally jump right in—holding one of your legs while you push, cheering you along, and giving you the play-by-play as the baby's head emerges. Some naturally stay up by your shoulders, helping you sit forward, talking into your ear, and giving you directions and encouragement.

Talk about where you think you'll need your spouse or partner to be and where he thinks he'll feel comfortable being.

Some spouses or partners don't have the desire or the capacity to see what's going on "down there" (even if you want them to), while others are glued to what's happening (even if you'd rather they *not* be). But you won't really know for sure until you're both experiencing the birth of your baby firsthand. Even so, it's a good idea to be on the same page beforehand. Talk about where you think you'll need him to be and where he thinks he'll feel comfortable being. It gives you the chance to iron out any sensitivities about what you do or don't want him to see and what he wants to see or is capable of seeing. This way, neither one of you is surprised or let down in the heat of the moment.

How Long Will You Push?

Be patient with yourself as you get your pushing rhythm down. It could take twenty to thirty minutes to figure out how to push effectively. And it will probably take much longer than that to push your baby out. On average, it takes first-time mothers one to two hours without an epidural and up to two or three hours with an epidural. But those are just the averages. Some women may need up to three or four hours, with or without an epidural. (Most of those stories you may have heard about babies being pushed out in minutes or, at the most, a half hour are from women who've already had babies.)

When progress is slow, it's common to get discouraged and feel that you're not doing it right. You are. It's just *your* version of right and that may take time.

Many first babies come down very gradually and progress is imperceptible as your baby makes its way through the different diameters of your pelvis. There's a real give-and-take that's happening now between your pelvis and your baby's head. It's really a matter of how your baby's head will mold to come through your pelvis and how much your pelvis will expand.

And then there are other factors that determine how long it will take, including physical ones—such as how exhausted you might be depending on how long you've been laboring, how big your baby is, or his or her position—or emotional ones, such as how ready you are to let go of pregnancy, which is a known, and become a mother, a complete unknown. When progress is slow, it's common to get discouraged and feel that you're not doing it right. You are. It's just *your* version of right and that may take time.

If Help Is Needed: Forceps and Vacuum

If you're exhausted and you don't have the strength to push, if an epidural isn't allowing you to feel the urge to push, if your baby needs to be maneuvered into a better position in order to come out, or if your baby is experiencing distress and needs to be delivered faster than you can push him or her—these are all situations in which your physician might consider using forceps or vacuum extraction.

While forceps have a scary reputation, it's a whole different deal nowadays. Your doctor will only consider a forceps delivery if your baby's head is low enough and he or she can be delivered easily. In vacuum extraction, a soft suction cup is placed on your baby's head and a hand pump creates just the right amount of suction so your doctor can help pull while you push. The choice whether to use forceps or vacuum is up to your physician, who bases it on which provides the least risk to your baby and is the best tool for the job. This is another one of those situations where it serves you well to have faith and trust in your doctor's expertise.

Here's generally how a forceps delivery or vacuum extraction goes: you may need a local or regional anesthetic and you may or may not need an episiotomy. As your doctor pulls from below, you push from above. Everybody's focused on one thing: getting the baby out.

Although an epidural may increase the chance for needing forceps or vacuum, most women can still deliver on their own, given enough time to push. As long as progress is being made and the baby is fine, time can really be an ally.

> *Linda: I had been pushing for four hours. So when they said, "The baby's coming!" I didn't buy it for a second. They had been telling me I was close for the last hour and now I was so tired I could barely push. Even though I was starting to feel some pressure through my epidural, I still didn't believe them. Then my midwife took my hand and put it between my legs and said, "Feel this, that's your baby's head. It's right there." I felt the top of a warm little head, and I was blown away! That was all I needed. I gave it everything I had.*

▪ Find Your Inspiration

If you get to the point where there's only a little bit more to go but you're exhausted and losing your oomph, a shot of inspiration may be just what you need when the going gets tough, as it can during pushing.

- **See your progress.** Ask for a mirror so you can watch your baby's head begin to emerge, or "crown."
- **Feel your progress.** Touch your baby's head, which is right there and means all you need is another push or two and he or she will be born.
- **Call it out.** If you don't know whether you're having a boy or girl, ask your delivery team to refrain from calling out your baby's sex. That way you and your spouse or partner can discover together your baby's sex and be the first to announce, "It's a boy!" or "It's a girl!"

The Crowning Glory

You'll know for sure that your baby's head is close to crowning when the hospital staff seems to move with an increased sense of purpose as they assume their respective positions around you and the room. The lights get turned up and the medical stuff that's been hidden away so as not to clash with the homey décor of your birthing room gets rolled out. If you haven't had an epidural, you'll know when your baby's head is crowning by the burning sensation you'll feel. Once you're fully stretched, it should feel less intense.

Episiotomy (the Uncut Version)

It's a fact that there are practitioners who perform episiotomies more frequently than others, and there are some who perform them routinely even though studies show that, in most women, it's best not to do an episiotomy. So if avoiding one is a big issue for you, find out beforehand where your practitioner falls. It's a great question to ask *before* signing on with a practice if it's a trigger point for you. And then during labor, way before you start pushing, remind your practitioner that you'd like to avoid an episiotomy. The key to minimizing tears is a gradual, slow delivery although sometimes that's not possible because of your baby's size or position.

The reasons for doing an episiotomy are pretty straightforward—to get a baby who might be in trouble out faster or if your perineum (the tissue between your vagina and rectum) isn't yielding enough. Practitioners who have a "wait-and-see" attitude about episiotomies will do one if these issues come up; otherwise they'll give your perineum time to stretch on its own so it can accommodate your baby's head without unnecessary surgery.

In the best of all worlds, you've talked to your doctor or midwife about your preferences way in advance of this moment, and you trust that he or she will make the best call for you depending on the circumstances. Remember, you hired this person for his or her medical expertise.

Here Comes Your Baby

As your pushes continue to guide your baby out, optimally, his or her head will be delivered slowly and gradually in order to reduce your chances for deep tearing and/or an episiotomy. To accomplish this you may be asked to resist the urge to push by breathing, blowing, or whatever it is you need to do instead.

> **Linda:** *My midwife told me to hold off pushing for a bit by chanting a slow, breathy "we" so I wouldn't tear. Then after my baby's head and shoulders came through, she again said, "Give me your hands." She guided them under my baby's arms and said, "The baby's right here. Pull your baby up to your belly. I'll help you." My husband who was up by my shoulders blurted out, "Honey, oh my God, we have a girl!" While I was still trying to recover from the thought that I had literally delivered my own baby, I think my husband was cutting the umbilical cord. I can't even remember. If you had asked me beforehand if I would have wanted to lift my baby out of me, I would have said, "Are you nuts?" But at that moment, it felt exactly right.*

Once your baby is born and everything is fine, he or she can often be placed right onto your belly and you can get some time to meet him or her before the hospital staff does all the weighing, measuring, footprinting, and so on. Your spouse or partner is offered the opportunity to cut the umbilical cord if he wants to. And if he doesn't, so be it. That doesn't make him any less of a person.

Next, your placenta detaches from the wall of your uterus like a pancake peeling off the inside of a balloon, and within five to twenty minutes after your baby is born, you push that out, which is nothing compared to pushing out your baby. If you've had a tear or an episiotomy, this is when your doctor or midwife does the repair.

> No matter how many babies are born every day all over the world, there are certain rites of passage that just are bigger than we know.

During these moments right after birth, while you watch them attend to your baby and as they attend to you, you take stock. No matter how many babies are born every day all over the world, there are certain rites of passage that just are bigger than we know. This is one of them. You did it.

· 12 ·

Cesarean Delivery

You may be hell-bent on avoiding one and planning to do whatever you can so you don't end up with one. Or, you'd rather *not* have one but you realize it depends on how well your labor goes and what your baby might need. Or, you may already be scheduled for one, either because it's medically necessary and what you need clinically or because it's exactly the way you want to have your baby, which falls under the heading of what you need psychologically.

Cesarean deliveries happen for many reasons. Some happen because of medical conditions that arise during pregnancy. Some result from what's happening or not happening in your labor or from what's happening for you or your baby. And some are planned, either because you've had a previous cesarean or just don't want a vaginal birth.

The thought of having a cesarean delivery brings up different feelings for different people. You may need very little emotional adjustment, if any, to the idea of it, particularly if it's your choice or even if it's medically necessary because that's the kind of person you are. On the other hand, you may be grappling with and trying to integrate the thought of having one and needing to do a lot of adjusting and processing. You could be experiencing a whole range of emotions—disbelief, disappointment, and resentment—not to mention feelings of failure and inadequacy, to name a few (as if that's not enough).

What Would Have Happened If . . . ?

In childbirth, just like in life, there's always the chance that events won't pan out the way you envisioned. (Which brings to mind the old adage "We make plans and God laughs.") If having a cesarean delivery is not that much of an emotional issue for you, there won't be as much at stake. But if it is, the aim of this chapter is to give you some hindsight in advance, so if you do end up having one you're not left with the unsettling question, "What would have happened if . . . ?" And you'll be less inclined to beat yourself up with the thought that maybe, just maybe, if *you* or *they* had done or tried something different, it could have changed things. That's not to say you can't feel disappointed or gypped out of the birth experience you had hoped for. You'll feel whatever you feel. And you need to have the space to feel those feelings. But ultimately you'll feel that everything that could have been done, was done.

> When you feel safe and supported and that your needs are being met, you set yourself up for the best possible birth experience—*because you are still giving birth.*

Here's the way to get that hindsight in advance. It's not about arming yourself with a slew of medical information or studies or statistics. Just ask yourself and your support team these four basic questions: Why is this happening? Can it be avoided and, if so, how? What can we try? Is trying that OK for both the baby and me? Then sift through all those answers until you're left with the ones that feel right. What you're willing or not willing to try. What feels comfortable. What feels uncomfortable. What feels risky. These answers will lead you to what you need to be doing in the moment, so at the other end you won't undermine the way things went and the decisions that were made.

Whether a cesarean happens during the course of labor or it's planned, the same principles hold true. When you feel safe and supported and that your needs are being met, you set yourself up for the best possible birth experience—*because you are still giving birth*. This chapter shows you how to do just that.

Why Cesarean Deliveries Are Done

A cesarean may be the best or only method for giving birth for a variety of reasons. Some have to do with you and some have to do with your baby. Or, it may simply be a personal choice.

Placenta Previa

In this situation, your placenta is literally blocking your cervix. There's no way for your baby to be born vaginally without interfering with his or her oxygen supply. This is one of the things checked for at your very first ultrasound. Here's a perfect example where a cesarean is a lifesaver.

Preecclampsia

No one knows what causes this trio of symptoms—high blood pressure, protein in your urine, and swelling (even more than you already have)—but a cesarean delivery could be necessary if your condition is severe and your cervix isn't favorable (not ready to dilate). Your doctor may want to deliver your baby as soon as it's far enough along developmentally in order to prevent your preeclampsia from getting worse. In most cases, once your baby is born, your blood pressure goes back to normal.

On the other hand, if your cervix *is* favorable and you're pretty far along in your pregnancy, an induction might be an alternative. Here's where the judgments of your physician and possibly a high-risk specialist come in.

Your Baby's Position

Your baby could just plain be in a wacky position: feet or bottom first (breech), sideways (transverse lie), or face forward, to name a few. Many doctors aren't trained anymore to deliver a breech baby vaginally because it's considered to be slightly riskier to the baby than when it's head first. An external version (rotating your baby into a head-down position by maneuvering your baby around from the outside of your abdomen) is an option. But there is still the chance that it won't work or he or she could flip back to breech, and to repeat the procedure may not be a clinically viable option or *you* might not opt to do it again.

Emergencies

While many TV shows would have you believe that emergency cesareans are a common occurrence, they're really not. But the truth is, it's still pretty dramatic when a baby is in trouble. Here again, a cesarean delivery can be lifesaving. If your doctor is concerned about changes in your baby's heart rate and attempts to get it back on track aren't working, a cesarean will be done if you're not close to delivering. A decision like this is usually made gradually after a period of careful monitoring. But sometimes it does happen suddenly. As anxiety-producing as that may be, the good news is that even with an emergency cesarean delivery, the chances are excellent that you and your baby will turn out just fine.

Personal Reasons

You may choose to have a cesarean delivery for a number of reasons that aren't deemed "medically necessary" but are very necessary to you. Maybe you had a difficult prior delivery and you don't want to go through that ever again. Or, you had a cesarean delivery previously and you don't want to take the chance of the small risk of uterine rupture or going through labor only to wind up with having another one. Perhaps you feel strongly about avoiding damage to your sexual, rectal, and bladder functions. You might be afraid of the pain of labor and delivery, and it causes you less anxiety to know exactly how and when you'll be giving birth. Decisions like these are usually made after talking at length with your doctor about your options and the pros and cons of an elective cesarean delivery. Sometimes a second opinion is helpful. But as always, the final decision is yours.

When Labor Doesn't Progress or Your Baby Stalls

Perhaps you're moving along just fine, you make it to five or six centimeters and then, no matter what you, your doctor, or your midwife do or try, your cervix doesn't budge another centimeter. Or, maybe you get to ten centimeters, but you've been pushing for hours and your baby's *still* not coming down.

You might not ever know exactly why your labor doesn't progress past a certain point or your baby doesn't descend. It could be any one or a combination of the following reasons. Your baby—because of his or her position or size (or both)—might not be able to make it through your pelvis. Maybe your contractions aren't strong or regular enough to dilate your cervix, even with the help of Pitocin.

What You Can Try

While it's impossible to predict ahead of time how much your pelvis will spread and how easily your baby will be able to maneuver its way down, there are variables you can play with to possibly help this situation along.

Position Changes to Help Shift Your Baby
- Squatting, which opens your pelvis to its widest diameter
- Lying on your back, which could give your baby the room it needs to get under your pubic bone
- Laboring on all fours
- Bouncing softly on a birth ball
- Rocking your hips back and forth
- If you have an epidural, being flipped gently from side to side by your labor support team

Other Options
- Rupturing your membranes if they're still intact and/or starting Pitocin to boost contractions
- Getting an epidural, if you haven't had one, which could give you a needed break and allow your cervix to dilate

Leave No Stone Unturned

In a situation where you're not dilating or your baby's not descending, you actually have the most latitude when it comes to trying whatever you feel you need to try in order to avoid a cesarean delivery—as long as your baby is doing fine with your labor and your practitioner is willing to go the distance with you.

Jessica: I was about a week past my due date and doing what I could on my own to get my labor going. We tried sex. I saw an acupuncturist a few times. And then, lo and behold, Wednesday morning my water broke and I thought, "Thank God!" I called my doctor to let him know and waited for my contractions to start. But hours went by and nothing happened. By six that night there was still nothing going on so I went into the hospital and my doctor put prostaglandin gel on my cervix to get things going. I woke up the next morning and still no contractions, so I got another dose of prostaglandin gel, and, because my chances for infection were increasing, I was started on Pitocin. And that's all it took. Hello, contractions. I went straight into coping mode. I was on the birth ball. I was in the shower. I was curled up in bed in the fetal position. But even though they kept upping the Pitocin, I was dilating at a snail's pace. I labored into the late afternoon until I was completely exhausted from dealing with the contractions. And then finally I got an epidural figuring if I could rest or sleep, maybe I'd dilate.

Because her baby wasn't in any distress, Jessica had the luxury of time to try what she felt she needed to avoid a cesarean delivery. But eventually, in situations like these, if progress isn't being made and options are exhausted, labor reaches an inevitable turning point. Sometimes the physician calls it. Sometimes a compromise is negotiated between physician and patient. And sometimes a woman calls it on her own.

Jessica: I was now four hours into my epidural and my cervix still hadn't moved. I never made it past six centimeters. My doctor said I could keep going, but I was done. There wasn't anything else I felt I could do or wanted to do. My baby wasn't coming down. I was tired from being at this for almost two days, and I was hungry. Now I just wanted my baby. They began prepping me for a cesarean delivery, and I was completely solid with it. When they lifted Will out of me and put him on the scale, he weighed in at a whopping nine pounds, eight ounces, and someone in the room said, "Say hello to your three-year-old!" I was thrilled, and when I replayed my delivery during the days and weeks afterward, there's not a single thing I would have changed. I completely understand why it happened, even though I did everything in my power to keep it from happening. I can live with that.

It also helped that Jessica's physician was attuned to how she wanted to give birth. He was able to counsel her from a place of expertise along with compassion for what Jessica wanted for herself. She felt supported as she processed what she did and didn't want to do to help her labor progress. The more processing you're able to do while you're in labor and possibly heading for a cesarean delivery, the less you'll need to do on the other side of it.

> Whether the birth of your baby by cesarean delivery is planned or unplanned, it can be as intimate and supportive an experience as you need it to be, even if it's taking place in an operating room.

It may also be helpful in the processing to consider that the body has ways of knowing things we can't yet see—what will and won't work; why labor isn't progressing; why the cervix isn't dilating; a baby who is not descending because of a shortened umbilical cord; a baby whose position won't allow it to descend; a baby whose size won't let it drop or come through the pelvis. The body really does have a kind of evolutionary, genetic, biological knowing. At some point, it comes down to trusting that.

Cesarean Delivery: Step by Step

Whether the birth of your baby by cesarean delivery is planned or unplanned, it can be as intimate and supportive an experience as you need it to be, even if it's taking place in an operating room. You can

■ **Cesarean Delivery: Good Birth Savvy**

- **Arrange for support.** If you have a doula, arrange in advance that she be permitted to stay with you during your delivery. This is a good idea whether you're scheduling a cesarean delivery or covering your bases just in case (some hospitals might not allow more than one person in the operating room). She'll support you and your partner during your delivery, and she can stay with you for the hour it takes to stitch you up while your spouse or partner goes to the newborn nursery with your baby.
- **Create the mood.** Bring in your tape/CD player and headset so you can listen to whatever you need to hear to keep you feeling OK.
- **Set the tone.** If you'd feel better knowing what's happening every step of the way or if you don't want to know anything about what's happening, just that your baby's OK, let your doctor know.
- **Find out on your own if it's a boy or girl.** If it's important for you and your partner to discover whether you have a boy or girl on your own, ask that you be allowed to do so as your baby is lifted above the screen. You can still make moments like these personal even in an operating room.

bring your music in. Most hospitals will allow your spouse or partner (or one person, whoever that is) to be there with you. If you don't know the sex of your baby, you can ask the operating room staff not to announce it so that you and your partner can discover it together.

Getting Ready

Typically, you'll be "prepped" for your cesarean delivery in your labor room. A bladder catheter and IV, if you don't have them already, are started and the top of your pubic area may be shaved. This is where

▪   A Spouse's—or Partner's—Guide to a Cesarean Delivery

Not every person is ready for a walk-on role on "ER," (whoops!) the OR. As always, the best kind of support you can give is the kind you're capable of giving. So if you don't think you can handle being in the operating room, speak right up. You're someone who knows your limits (and that's actually a *good* thing!).

Once they've wheeled your spouse or partner off to surgery to start prepping her, you'll be left alone in the labor room to put on your scrubs, booties, and surgical mask. If you need help figuring out the garb (and want to save yourself the humiliation of walking into surgery with a bootie on your head) or you're just feeling anxious, head over to the nurse's station. You can talk to the nurses about what to expect in the operating room or, at the very least, get some tips on how to put on your surgical attire.

In the operating room, you'll sit right at your spouse's or partner's head and you can talk to her, hold her head, and stroke her hair. You won't be able to see the surgery (but you can ask if you want to) because there will be a screen in front of her chest. It only takes about five to ten minutes to get your baby out, and, after you've had some time together, the three of you—you, a nurse, and your baby will all head to the newborn nursery.

your "bikini" incision will be made (how you'll look in one after surgery is probably not high on your list at this moment). If your delivery is scheduled, this prep part might proceed at a manageable pace. If your delivery is happening during the course of labor, this prep part might feel hurried, especially if a cesarean delivery wasn't part of your plan. If it's not an emergency, ask everybody to slow down, if possible, so you have time (if you need it) to acclimate and process what's happening. You still may be trying to cope with contractions even though you're headed for surgery. You may need extra support to manage those last contractions until your epidural is boosted or begun.

In the OR

Once you're in the operating room, an epidural or spinal is started or your epidural is boosted if you already had one. Your anesthesiologist is right there at your head. Your doctor will drape the area to create a sterile field around your belly. You won't be able to see what's happening because of the screen in front of your chest, but once your baby is born they'll lift her or him above it so you can get your first glimpse.

While your cesarean delivery is happening, let your anesthesiologist and doctor know what you need to hear—whether it's a play-by-play of the entire delivery, lots of reassurance that the baby is fine, or nothing because you need to zone out ("just let me know when the baby's here"). Remember, even though they're all completely at home in an OR, you're probably not—and you're the one having major abdominal surgery.

Here Comes Your Baby

Once your surgery begins, you shouldn't feel any pain but you'll probably feel pressure, pulling, tugging, and/or pushing. It's a really strange feeling actually, but it can take a lot of maneuvering to get your baby dislodged from your pelvis and out through that small incision. What's truly amazing is that it only takes about five minutes or so to get to your baby, lift it out, and hold it up for you to see. He or she then gets handed to the pediatric nurse, checked out, weighed, cleaned up a bit, and wrapped up into a tight little package and delivered into your spouse's or partner's arms. Your partner can then put your baby right up to your cheek. *Your baby.* And the three of you can take some time to take it all in—pictures, smelling, talking, crying (and maybe even some nausea from the anesthesia and shaking, which is a natural reaction to giving birth).

After you get some time with your baby, he or she will leave the operating room to get a thorough checkup and cleanup in the newborn nursery. Your spouse or partner usually goes with your baby and that leaves you and the next and longer part of the story—your repair.

After removing your placenta, your doctor stitches you up for the next thirty minutes to an hour. During your repair, it's possible to feel nauseous and have the shakes. Rely on the people who are there with you to get you through it. If you're feeling nauseous, unnerved, or panicky from the shaking and can't relax, you have but to ask and your anesthesiologist can give you medication to stop the nausea and/or medication through your IV so you can relax and doze.

Once your incision is repaired, you are brought into your recovery room so your vital signs can be monitored, and you're reunited with your spouse or partner and baby. If you plan on breast feeding, and you feel up to it, your nurse or doula will help you. Then after a couple of hours in recovery, you are brought into your postpartum room.

The Road to Recovery

Remember, you've just had major abdominal surgery, so it's pretty likely that you're going to need some pain medication. How much you'll need depends on how much pain you're in. If you're breast-feeding and worried about it getting to your baby, time your medication. Take it right after you breast-feed so it won't be at its peak for the next feeding. And since you don't actually produce milk these first few days, your baby is getting only a small amount of the first substance your breasts produce—anitbody-rich colostrum (further minimizing the amount of pain medication that gets to your baby). It's perfectly safe to use pain medication for the first week or so after your delivery. It doesn't do you or your baby any good to try to tough it out if you're in a lot of pain. You need to be comfortable enough in order to relax so your milk comes in.

Within twenty-four hours your IV and catheter will be removed so you can get up and move around. You may not be quite prepared for how much your movement stems from your center, where that surgery took place. You may be on stool softeners until you've had your first bowel movement. That way you won't have to use your abdominal muscles so much when you push. (That's usually the time when you swear that nothing will ever come into or go out of your body ever again.)

> While you're in it, begin at the end. Ask yourself what you need to do so when it's all said and done you're not left second-guessing yourself, your doctor, or the circumstances.

But actually, there is something that you'll very much want to get out of your body: gas. It has built up in your intestines because of your surgery and it will make its presence known as it tries to get out. For some, the pain from the gas can be worse than the pain from the incision. Getting up and moving around with the help of your nurse can alleviate it. So can a heating pad and sometimes a laxative. But mostly it just takes a little time.

There are some sure signs you might be ready to leave the hospital. For instance, when it starts to feel like instead of trying to heal you they're actually trying to drive you crazy. Or, you can't sleep because your nurse wakes you up every time she checks in on you and then just when you're drifting off, you're jarred awake by the sounds of "paging Dr. Blah-Blah-Blah." You can't stomach one more bite of the hospital food and you just want your own bed and the surroundings and smells of home. Or, maybe you feel like you *never* want to leave. You and your baby's needs are completely taken care of, and you've gotten quite used to being served breakfast, lunch, and dinner in bed. And blankets straight from the warmer are pure heaven. Following are some tips to help you make this transition from hospital to home.

Good Birth Savvy: Cesarean Delivery Recovery

- **Establish guidelines for visitor etiquette.** Yes, you've had a baby and people want to wish you well but try not to skip over the fact that you've just had surgery. Also add into the equation the possibility that you labored for however many hours *before* you had your cesarean delivery. You might not feel like or even be able to entertain visitors right away and that's really OK. If you're dealing with sadness and disappointment over not having a vaginal delivery, give yourself the time and space you need to feel what you're feeling without having to "put on a happy face" for visitors. And if there's some immediate ritual party necessary, such as a bris, have other people do the brunt of the work—it may very well be the next lesson in the lineup of learning to relinquish control and prioritizing so you can take care of you and your baby. Do what you need to do for you. Everyone will get to see you and your baby eventually.

- **Get help.** It's pretty much essential that you have help for at least a couple of weeks, whether it's family, friends, or the hired kind. How long and how much help you need will depend on your recovery and your circumstances.

- **Heal thyself.** Your body will heal in its own time and in its own way. And again, how long you labored before your delivery will also factor into your healing process. You'll most likely be able to walk around and eat regular food as soon as you feel like it or, with some practitioners, within twelve to twenty-four hours, and leave the hospital in three to four days. Try to avoid comparing yourself to others. You've just had a baby *and* major surgery. Maybe your neighbor was back to running two weeks after her cesarean delivery (thanks so much for sharing) and you're wondering how that is possible when you can't even get it together to take a walk. Give yourself whatever time you need to heal.

Processing a Cesarean Delivery: Begin at the End

Some time ago the phrase "A birth from above, instead of a birth from below" was coined and applied like a Band-aid, disregarding that there were women who were grappling with disappointment about their cesarean deliveries. But the truth of the matter is, many women who've had a cesarean delivery, and even those who made it their mission to avoid one, are looking back at them from a place of confidence instead of regret. So for those of you who wind up needing a cesarean delivery, here's the way to feel good about yourself and the experience.

While you're in it, begin at the end. Ask yourself what you need to do so when it's all said and done you're not left second-guessing yourself, your doctor, or the circumstances. This bit of forethought may very well save you from feeling bad at the other end. It doesn't mean that maybe you won't feel disappointed or mourn what you didn't have. But if you labor in a way that feels right for you, you feel like you're part of the decision-making team, and you feel supported, you're much less likely to feel like you had an unnecessary cesarean delivery. And you won't be left with the unsettling feeling that if only *you* or *they* "ran faster" or "jumped higher" it wouldn't have ended up this way. It may not have ended up the way you wished it would have, but not only can you can live with that, you can feel good about yourself around it. Aside from your and your baby's health, that's what truly matters.

· 13 ·

After Your Baby Is Born

You've labored for however many hours. You've pushed your baby out or he or she has been lifted out of your body. Now comes the moment when you lay eyes on this little person who's been growing inside you all these many months. This once figment of your imagination is now a wriggling, slippery—maybe even wailing—real live baby. What will you be feeling? What are you even *supposed* to be feeling?

I Love You, I Love You Not

Just as there's no one right way to give birth to your baby, there's no single right way to feel when you meet your baby for the first time. You could fall in love instantly. The primal faucet gets turned on full force. You can't remember what life was like two minutes ago when this baby was still in your body, and you're blown away by how powerful your feelings are.

And then again, you might be taken aback or even alarmed if you don't feel that way. You might be exhausted and still reeling from your birth experience and need some time to decompress and take it all in. You might need some time to get to know your baby. After all, how *do* you fall in love with someone you've just met?

If this isn't your first baby, you might be thinking, "OK, he's very cute. I'm happy to nurse him, but when are his real parents coming to pick him up?" After all, you already *have* your family.

Like most everything about birth, you can't predict how you're going to feel when they place that baby on your chest. But just know this, how you feel about her or him during this one moment in time is not going to make or break your potential ranking in the mothering department. You will be a mother for the rest of your life; the fact that you are even reading this book means that you'll probably be a very good one, too. Whether the connection at birth is instant or not, your relationship with your baby builds over time. Gazing into each other's eyes and nuzzling after a diaper change, smelling the sweet clean scent of his little head as he's asleep in your arms, finally getting her to stop crying and fall asleep after a hard night of rocking and swaying her from room to room— this is the stuff of motherhood.

> Just as there's no one right way to give birth to your baby, there's no single right way to feel when you meet your baby for the first time.

Expectation Revisitation

Just as there's a lot of pressure during pregnancy to be the "gotta do it right" pregnant woman—eat the right foods, stay away from the wrong ones (oh no, was there feta in that salad?!), avoid the litter box, play Mozart for your baby's developing brain, and so on and so on, it's no different after you give birth, except now you'll feel pressure to be the "gotta do it right" mother.

That pressure will come from just about everyone including *you*. That never-ending barrage of advice about what's best for your baby flows as torrentially now as when you were pregnant. But now you're doubly vulnerable because, instead of being a mere notion of things to come, this baby is a reality—a person for whom you are *completely* responsible. That could be a confidence shaker considering you don't have a track record yet to know that you really do have what it takes to be a good mother. But you do. And the things you don't know now, you'll figure out. The job of motherhood involves learning a whole new set of skills while pretty much flying by the seat of your pants. (Where *were* all those courses on how to deal with sleep deprivation and being in constant demand?) Just as with any new job, be patient with yourself and give yourself the time you need to learn.

Here's your reality check. Go back to your expectations (remember those?)—the ones that truly reflect you, the ones that are everyone else's, the ones that you think you should have, and the ones that don't take into account that things might go differently than you think they will. Run them through the sandbox sifter, so to speak. What remains are your true expectations—everything that's right and true about *you*. The same way that they are your road markers through childbirth, they are your road markers as a mother.

> The job of motherhood involves learning a whole new set of skills while pretty much flying by the seat of your pants.

Motherhood is an ever-evolving process. Sometimes you'll feel like it's smooth sailing. And sometimes you'll feel like you're lost at sea. But there's a tried-and-true course for regaining your footing— always refer back to *you*. To do that, trust your instincts, taking whatever advice works for you *and* your baby and passing on what doesn't. Accept yourself for who you are instead of trying to be someone you're not and be flexible about changing what you're doing or reevaluating your mind-set if it isn't working. This is mothering from your true north.

Bonding or Bondage?

Most of the pressures that might come your way right at birth pretty much center on the "mother-infant" bond. Whatever it is that you already know about that bond, you can be sure by the time you're close to giving birth, you'll have gotten an earful more on the subject. You may start feeling pressed to make decisions that maybe you never even knew you had to make. Should I ask them to hold off on the antibiotic eye ointment so he can see me clearly right after birth? If you're breast-feeding, should I nurse her immediately? Do I want "rooming in"? You might be worried that if you make the "wrong" choices, you'll ruin your chances of ever bonding with your baby or at the very least, the connection between you won't be as strong as it could be. The pressure to be an "Über-parent" starts even before your baby is born, and it can be tricky not to get caught up in the frenzy because, of course, you want to be the best parent you can be. But if what you're hearing about bonding is making you feel more like you're in bondage to someone *else's* idea of what's right, take that as a sign that it's not right for you. Use that self-feedback as your guide when it comes to making choices along the way.

Are You My Mother?

It's hospital routine to give babies antibiotic eye ointment shortly after they're born to prevent eye infections. You'll probably find out in childbirth class that babies are very alert for an hour or so after birth and you can choose to delay this ointment so your baby can see you clearly in order to bond "effectively." Some childbirth educators tend to get whipped into a froth about this one, but the truth is delaying the ointment is no big deal. Hospitals aren't conspiring

---

▪ **Are You My Baby?**

Footprinting right after birth used to be the fail-safe way of making sure the right baby wound up with the right mother. Not to fret, you'll still be handed those sweet little prints but, in these high-tech days, footprinting is pretty much a matter of memorabilia. The high-tech version is that right after birth your baby gets two coded ID bands (usually one for the wrist and one for the ankle) and you and your spouse or partner get bands that match your baby's.

---

to stop babies from bonding with their mothers at birth. It's simply a matter of letting your nurse know that you'd like some time with your baby before she administers the ointment. They're quite used to the request and it's usually not an issue. Should you happen to forget or find out after the fact, try not to worry. Your baby won't be wandering around like the storybook bird that hatches while his mother is out of the nest and starts asking dogs, cows, and planes, "Are you my mother?" You and your baby have your whole lives to bond.

Breast Feeding or Breast Fascism?

Breast feeding shortly after birth is mostly an issue of supply and demand. The theory is that the sooner your baby nurses, the sooner your milk will come in and by introducing your baby to your breast (think of it as an initial "meet and greet"), you encourage that to happen. But as many new mothers can attest, the window of opportunity for successful breast feeding is a lot more open than just that.

If you're planning on breast feeding and *want* to nurse right after your baby is born, then go for it. Just keep in mind that it's also about what's right for your baby. He or she may latch on immediately or not show the slightest interest. Does that mean you're a breast-feeding failure? Not a chance. Remember, it's also about what's right for you. Maybe you don't feel like nursing right away because you're wiped out and need some time to *take care of yourself*. (Repeat that slowly three times.) Or, maybe it just gets lost in the shuffle because you and your spouse or partner are completely caught up in the moment.

> *Janice: Bryan was born just before midnight after eighteen hours of labor. When they put him on my chest I was just so elated that he was here and he was OK and it was over, that I didn't even think about nursing him. My husband and I couldn't believe how alert he was. He was look-ing around taking it all in. We just stared into his eyes and talked to him for what seemed the longest time before the nurses took him to clean him up and I got cleaned up and had something to eat. After they wheeled him back into my room, he was sound asleep and before you know it, so was I. The next morning a lactation nurse showed me how to breast-feed him and he got it immediately, latching on like a hungry little tiger. I have to say I was surprised at how smoothly it went right from the start. Lots of what I had heard or read about breast feeding and all the vari-ables that can lead to its success or failure kind of left me anxious, think-ing that maybe I wouldn't be able to do it or that my baby might not take to it. But we did just fine.*

Not every newborn latches on as easily as Bryan, and not every new mother finds getting started as easy as Janice did. Even when it does go without a hitch, the path to breast feeding can be paved with issues like sore nipples, engorgement, how your baby's digestive sys-tem reacts to what you're eating, and how you feel about being open for business 24/7. You might need some help ironing out the wrin-kles, or even some heavy creases. It could take a while to figure out a system that works for both of you, but one thing's for sure, the two of you will have plenty of time to get the hang of nursing.

Breast, Bottle, Both?

Deciding how you want to feed your baby might feel like one of the biggest decisions you have to make as a newborn mother. Particularly since what essentially should be *your* decision, seems to have become everyone else's business. You're bound to have heard (it's kind of hard not to—it's everywhere) that "breast is best" for your baby. But it's only "best" for your baby if it's also "best" (or something close to that) for you. Breast feeding is not only about nutrition and health. It's also about finding the balance between what you want for the baby, what's right for you, and how all of it actually fits into your life. What that might look like will be different for everyone.

> Breast is only "best" for your baby if it's also "best" (or something close to that) for you.

You may be completely committed to breast feeding right from the start. Or maybe you're not sure, but you're open to giving it a try. You might be thinking about doing just the first few days—the immunities from the colostrum are big for you—but that'll probably be it. Maybe your plan is to breast-feed and start pumping as soon as possible so that: A. Your spouse or partner can feed the baby, too; B. You can get a break and/or get some sleep; C. Somebody else can take care of the baby so both of you can get a break; or D. Something even far more radical—so you can just have dinner together and talk. Maybe you've got to get the baby on a bottle because you're going back to work in a few months. Perhaps you'll bypass pumping completely and supplement with formula (gasp!). Or maybe, just maybe, you'll go right to formula. Breast feeding is not for you.

One thing you can be sure of. No matter what you do, somebody's going to have something to say about it. And to add insult to injury, figuring out the feeding thing can put you in even more of a vulnerable place because it's steeped in trial and error. You may go through five different kinds of formula before you find the one that doesn't cause your baby to projectile puke across the room. Or, you may need more support and reassurance than you ever realized because breast feeding isn't as natural for you as you thought it would be.

Put everything through that sandbox sifter once again when deciding how you want to feed your baby. Once your baby's born, use the very same formula (no bias intended) if you need to rethink or revamp your decision. Ask yourself:

- Are your expectations realistic?
- Are they your own—not your mother's, your sister's, or your best friend's?
- Are you doing it because you feel like you "should"?
- If it's not going the way you thought it would, are you flexible about trying something different and clear on just how far you're willing to go to make it work?

The bottom line is there's really no one right way to feed your baby.

Shannon: I was definitely planning on breast-feeding. Even before my baby was born I took a breast-feeding class so I would be prepared. I had the La Leche League "bible"—The Womanly Art of Breastfeeding—and I got a "My Brest Friend" nursing pillow as a shower gift. I was so ready. I nursed Sally right after she was born, and the next day I had a session with the hospital's lactation nurse. She seemed to be nursing great. We went home and everything went well although it really got to be a struggle to get her to stay awake at my breast. At her first checkup that Monday we found out that she had dropped weight. My pediatri-

cian was concerned and wanted me to start supplementing with formula. I was so sad but so torn. I wanted to breast-feed my baby but I was scared that she wasn't gaining weight. I got a recommendation for a lactation consultant and called her right away. She came over and we discovered that Sally didn't really have such a great latch so she showed me some ways to make it stronger, which in turn would hopefully increase my milk supply. She showed me how I could use this thing called a supplemental nursing system, which would let me keep nursing but get Sally some formula. I taped a tiny tube onto my breast that was attached to what looked like a small IV bag filled with formula, which hung around my neck. So every time I nursed Sally, she got formula along with my breast milk. Then, in order to boost my milk supply, I needed to pump in between feedings. After the lactation consultant left, my husband and I looked at each other in a complete daze. It seemed like out of a twenty-four-hour day, I was going to need forty-eight hours just to feed my baby and increase my milk supply. That was so not the way I pictured it would be.

How does Shannon's story end? Put yourself in her shoes and finish it according to the right ending for you. Here are some possible variations:

- With her husband Jack's help, Shannon continues with the supplemental nursing system. Their routine during the week that he's off from work goes like this: Jack soothes the baby while Shannon gets everything set up and tapes the feeding tube to her breast. She nurses. Jack burps and changes the baby and puts her down in her bassinet. Shannon then pumps both breasts for half an hour in order to boost her milk supply (thankfully she has the double pump!). She crawls back into bed and then repeats the system an hour and a half later when Sally wakes up. By the time Jack goes back to work, Sally is slowly gaining weight and Shannon is able to cut down the supplemental nursing system to twice a day. Within a month she's nursing exclusively.

- Shannon comes to the decision that adding the supplemental nursing system is just too overwhelming. She decides that she will continue to nurse Sally, that she will pump in between feedings to boost her milk supply, and that Jack will "top off" Sally with some formula, once in the morning and once at night, after she nurses. By her next checkup, Sally hasn't gained weight, but she hasn't lost any more. Shannon and Jack step up the routine to full formula bottles twice a day and Shannon nurses in between. The combination works and Sally starts to gain weight. By the time she's about three months old it's clear that she prefers the formula bottles but still likes to be nursed right before bedtime. Although breast feeding didn't end up the way she thought it would, it's a balance that Shannon can live with.

- Shannon decides, with Jack's support, that jumping through hoops to breast-feed and the extra anxiety about the baby's weight gain is not worth it. She and Jack start Sally on formula bottles and she gobbles them down with gusto, regaining the weight she lost in just a few days. Although Shannon is disappointed that breast-feeding didn't work out, it's more important to her that Sally is gaining weight without the drama that might have come from continuing to breast-feed.

The decision about whether to breast-feed, supplement, or go straight to a bottle is the start of the parenting balancing act—balancing your needs, your limits, and your vision of how you want to parent with your baby's needs. Just as these three possible story endings show, everyone's balance is different and only you can determine when you've struck the right one. There are plenty of experts, family members, and friends who will tell you what's best for your baby—quoting the latest research and all. But if it doesn't work for you and you end up feeling resentful, that can't possibly be good for either of you. The surefire way to get to what's right for you comes from looking at your choices, weighing the pros and cons, and figuring out what comes closest to what you want. Then if it's still not working, move on, preferably without beating yourself up over it.

Rooming In or Give Me Some Room?

Rooming in has to do with the two "Bs"—bonding and breast-feeding. According to the experts, having your baby with you in your hospital room instead of in the newborn nursery sets off a chain reaction that helps reinforce both of them: you learn how to read your baby's hunger cues and nurse "on demand," which causes your breast milk to come in. The theory is, if your baby is in the newborn nursery and gets served up a bottle or a pacifier, the supply-and-demand process could be undermined and your baby might be afflicted with the dreaded (*heavy pause*) "nipple confusion."

Whether you breast-feed or not and where your baby stays depends on *your* needs. You may want your baby with you around the clock because that's what feels right to you. Or, you may want your baby with you because you're worried that she'll scream her head off unattended in the newborn nursery, or if you're breast-feeding, that they'll give her a bottle. You can always make your preferences known and ask for reassurance that that won't be the case. But it's not going to do you any good to sit in your room knotted with tension, worrying about what might be going on in the newborn nursery. Keep her with you if that's what you need to feel safe and comfortable.

On the other hand, the newborn nursery may be a godsend if you're exhausted and want to sleep but would feel better if someone was keeping an eye on your baby. It could very well be the best babysitting you'll ever have, with trained pediatric nurses round the clock. (Down the road, there will be times at 3 A.M. when you're stumbling to another feeding that you may think longingly about that newborn nursery.) If you're breast-feeding, you can ask your nurse to bring your baby into your room whenever he wakes up. And if you're worried they'll give your baby a bottle or pacifier, put a note in his bassinet that reminds them not to.

Your baby will be rooming in for the next eighteen years (or more!) of his or her life. When you look back, those first few days in the hospital may well seem like a blip on the radar screen. Base your decision on where your baby stays on what you need during this particular moment in time. You can choose to take advantage of the help that's there for you, or not, if you don't need or want it.

First the Ecstasy, Then the Laundry

The moment of parenting truth comes once your hospital stay is over and you get to bring your baby home. The fantasy of what you thought it would be like meets up with reality. Those first few days at home will find you pretty much immersed in your baby. Life as you used to know it will fade into the outskirts of this new life. Your focus will be on figuring out what the cries mean, working out the feeding part, swaddling, changing diapers, rocking, and maybe tending to the baby laundry that quickly piles up. Your days will no longer be divided into morning and night. They'll cycle continuously around the clock, one day indistinguishable from the next, driven by feedings and maybe two- to three-hour stretches of sleep. This is life with a newborn. You will be on baby time.

During these first few days and weeks you may feel completely and utterly consumed—by the feelings you have for your baby *and* by the demands of newborn motherhood. Being responsible for another human being who's dependent on you for everything is a huge job. And however hard you fall for your baby, you may mourn the life you had before, when you had time to take care of you and it was just "the two of you." (Remember your spouse or partner? Remember back to that time before you started feeling like a character on "Desperate Housewives" and he like Jack Nicholson in *The Shining*?) While pregnancy offers you nine months of getting used to the idea of having a baby, nothing prepares you for the reality of it. Once there, you and your emotions hit the ground running, and it could take some time for your head to catch up with this new and very different life.

Picking Up the Pieces (and Still the Laundry)

Eventually, the fog of the first few days will lift (maybe because you have a night where you get more than three hours of uninterrupted sleep) and you'll realize that all of those other things you used to do *before* you had a baby—and we're talking just the basics here like laundry, shopping, cooking, and so on—somehow need to be worked back into the picture. It probably won't be any consolation to remember that you *used* to do all those things plus hold down a job; be an attentive friend, sister, daughter, wife, or partner; have a social life; *and* get to the gym. It's entirely possible that you may barely be able to find the time to bathe, let alone cook a meal. The sheer magnitude of having to work back in all those everyday things could send you right over the edge.

So if you can (and this will depend on how much of a control freak you are), take it one chore at a time and give yourself permission to relax your standards. Managing to get the laundry clean and dry, even if it's still sitting unfolded in the basket, is a huge accomplishment. You might never even get to the folding part, let alone put the clothes away in drawers. They'll go directly from the basket onto your body and that's how it will work for now until you can manage more.You might discover that folded clothes are highly overrated and maybe you'll be able to let it go even longer because at this time your plate is pretty darn full.

Motherhood 101

You'll be able to do a *certain* amount of prep work and setup before your baby's born—things like figuring out when you'll stop working, getting your baby's room in order, arranging for and coordinating the help you'll need after your baby's born, and so on. But no matter how organized and prepared you are, there's just no predicting what it will be like and how you'll feel when you bring your baby home.

There's the caretaking stuff to figure out. It might take some time to get the hang of holding this tiny, fragile creature with a head that wobbles like it's attached to a spring and a startle reflex that startles *you*. Or, you may find yourself actually breaking into a sweat, heart pounding, as you struggle to diaper your baby as he shrieks like he's being tortured on the changing table.

Then there's all the emotional stuff that plays into it, like what kind of mother you want to be. How *you* were mothered feeds into how you want to do it differently and/or the realization that your mother did a lot that was right! You may even discover that you are a lot *like* your mother. Be patient with yourself as you learn the skills of mothering. The learning curve is particularly steep because there's no way to learn how to do it until you're actually doing it.

A Mother Unlike Any Other

Everyone will have their own opinions on the best or hardest parts of being a mother. The point to remember is that they're talking about the "best" or "hardest" parts for *them*, which is based on their likes, dislikes, hopes, and fears.You'll be a mother unlike any other because your mothering will be shaped by your own unique set of likes, dislikes, hopes, and fears. It might turn out that what you find extremely difficult, your mother saw as a piece of cake. (And you're left wondering how on earth did she pull it off?) Your best friend might not understand why you would use cloth diapers when disposables are "so much less of a hassle." Your sister might "break it to you" that "your next vacation with your spouse or partner will be after your kid goes to college." That might be true for them, but only you know what's true for you.

> You'll be a mother unlike any other because your mothering will be shaped by your own unique set of likes, dislikes, hopes, and fears.

How you mother also depends on your baby. Every little one comes with its own distinct personality. Your coworker might have fond memories of hanging out for hours at the local coffee shop, reading the paper and meeting up with friends while her baby napped contentedly in his stroller. Your baby, on the other hand, might not be able to take all that stimulation and cry inconsolably the entire time until you get her home. Babies come in all different shapes, sizes, and temperaments. Some roll with the punches and others thrive on routine. Some are smiley and huggable and others are serious and observant. Just like tapping into what's right for you in labor and delivery, take the same approach when it comes to meeting your baby's needs. Tap into what you think is right for her or him.

You'll typically hear that the first six weeks of newborn motherhood are the hardest. That's because it will take about that amount of time, and sometimes longer, for your baby to start settling into a routine and sleeping for longer stretches at night. And at the same time you're adjusting, too, both mentally and physically. Your body is recovering from pregnancy and birth, and you're dealing with the superhuman demands of taking care of your baby and maybe coming to grips with the fact that it's impossible to "do it all."

Advice abounds (printed and spoken) about making it through that immediate newborn period. Take care of you by tailoring those traditional words of wisdom to meet *your* needs. As usual, take what works and take a pass on what doesn't.

New-Mom Tips with a Personal Twist

One of the things mothers do best is network and problem-solve—sharing ideas and tips on just about everything. Think of that sharing as a banquet table loaded up with gifts of wisdom—some of which you'll decline, some of which will be exactly what you need. Here's a sampling of that wisdom.

- **Seek help.** Getting help during the first few weeks is essential, but only the kind that's helpful to *you*. The last person you need to be taking care of is your "caretaker." Your options range from enlisting family and friends to hiring a baby nurse or doula (who will not only take care of the baby but also take care of you, plus run errands, cook, do laundry, etc.). Get creative to fit your needs and budget. If having your out-of-town mother or mother-in-law stay with you is going to drive you crazy, put her up with family or check out the possibility of a hotel. Instead of baby gifts, ask for meals, laundry service, errand running, or a few hours of babysitting so you can have a little bit of time for you.

- **Rest when the baby naps.** If you're the kind of person who can pull this off, it really can make a difference in the sleep deprivation department. If you're the kind of person who needs to be chained down in order to sit still and you've never taken a nap in your grown-up life, start small. Consider resting or flipping through a magazine for at least *one* of your baby's naps. And stop beating yourself up that you should be folding laundry. Even if you feel you're managing fine on less sleep, try not to skimp on downtime. Sleep deficits tend to catch up with you sooner or later.

- **Set up your space.** If you have two floors, set up a diaper-changing area on each one, especially if you've had a cesarean. It can be as simple as filling a basket with a few diapers, wipes, and a changing pad. If you're on the phone a lot, go portable with a belt clip and headset. It's pretty hard to juggle a phone and feed an infant for any length of time. (Plus you'll prevent yourself from becoming a chiropractor's fantasy.) Keep bottled water wherever you feed or nurse your baby. This is especially important if you're breast-feeding, in order to replenish what you're putting out. And if you have more than one floor, keep a nursing pillow on each one (you can always borrow or buy a spare, secondhand pillow).

- **Redefine visitor etiquette.** If you need your privacy and/or time to yourselves—guard that vigilantly. Plan to limit or stagger visitors, and put a cap on visiting time so your energy isn't sapped. This might bring on some guilt because everyone will be genuinely eager to meet your baby. But it might help to look at it this way: you'll need to be taking care of you because you'll have a baby to take care of. And about those thank-you notes. You may be wondering, if you can't even find the time to change your sanitary pad, how will you find the time to write 324 thank-you notes? Go easy on yourself. Maybe write one a day or a few a week. You'll feel like you're accomplishing something and sooner or later you'll get to the bottom of your list. (Wouldn't it be a real gift to new mothers that, along with the baby gift, there's no need for a thank-you note? Everybody just assumes your gratitude.)

If I'm So Happy, Why Am I Crying?

Even if you're head over heels in love with your baby, it's normal to have some feelings of sadness during the first weeks. Life with a new baby is extremely challenging and can feel isolating. There's less time for you and less time for you as a couple *away* from your baby. Hormonal fluctuations as your body readjusts to its prepregnant state could intensify these feelings even more, making you feel like you're on an emotional roller coaster. Thankfully, your ride should be short-lived once your hormones settle down and you find your rhythm as a new mother. With each element of this adjustment period, be good to yourself. Give yourself the right to stumble and feel whatever you feel; be patient while you find your way.

Beyond the Blues

If your emotions start to feel exceedingly overwhelming, debilitating, and/or they affect the way you feel about or care for your baby, that's a sign that it's more than the baby blues. Symptoms of postpartum depression can include seesawing from "high" to "low": crying jags; feeling so sad or numb that you can barely make it through the day; experiencing anxiety, panic attacks, loss of appetite, or insomnia; feeling angered or irritated by your baby's cries; and feeling afraid that you're going to hurt your baby or yourself. It's common to feel guilty or ashamed of what you're feeling—that you're not living up to "supermom" standards or that you're a "bad" mother. But don't let that get in the way of getting the help you need. Postpartum depression has nothing to do with the quality of your mothering. It's a biological reaction to having just been pregnant and given birth, and it requires treatment. Therapy, support groups, and medication (yes, even if you're nursing) can successfully treat postpartum depression. See your physician or OB-GYN and ask for a referral to a psychiatrist, psychologist, or therapist who specializes in treating postpartum depression.

The Mommy Network

There's no one else who will *really* get what you're going through like other newborn moms. The relief that you may feel, for example, when you find out that another mother in your mother's group also didn't experience that postbirth high that everyone talks about can make you feel really normal. You can get that same kind of relief from chatting online and finding out that you're not the only one worrying about everything. (Postings cover the gamut, from the color of poop [there we go again!] to the pros and cons of pacifiers.) You'll learn a lot from other mothers' success and horror stories. Plus you'll be able to share your own and get some much needed support, feeling much less isolated in the process. Ask for leads on mothers' groups at your pediatrician, OB-GYN, or midwife's office, tap into your doula's resources, inquire at your local Y, or ask around at your new mommy exercise or yoga classes. Check out online parenting sites for groups in your area and chat rooms with other mothers.

Bringing Up Baby

You've actually been making decisions about your baby's well-being from the moment you found out you were pregnant. Maybe you've passed on that cup of coffee or glass of wine or made the best of bed rest because your baby's health depends on it. And soon will come the day when the shadowy black-and-white sonogram image (which looks sort of like an amoeba) on your refrigerator transforms into a real baby. *Your* baby. There in your arms will be living proof of what you are meant to do: take care of this boy or this girl the best way you know how, even though you may not have any idea *how*.

There are so many decisions to be made right from the beginning. Your baby won't even have been cleaned off and everyone will be asking you his or her name. Then there are such issues as cord blood banking, newborn screening, circumcision, inoculations, co-sleeping—just to name a few. You'll find yourself figuring out answers and making choices in the face of sometimes fierce pressure from experts who are essentially strangers, as well as family members and friends you hold close to your heart. This is the beginning of a long list of decisions that you will make as you chaperone your child to his or her adult years.

But your sandbox sifter is always there at the ready: Does this fit who you are? Does this fit what you want for your baby? Are you doing it because of social pressure? Are you doing it because you think you *should* be doing it? And the ultimate last question: Do you feel good about this decision? As always, lots of people will have lots of opinions on whatever it is you do—starting pretty much immediately—from the name you give your baby all the way up to what college they should attend and beyond. All that matters is that *you* know you are making decisions with confidence and with so much love for your child. And isn't that what we all want as parents? To love our babies and give them the gift of self-esteem so they in turn can depend on their own personal sandbox sifters as they make their way through the world.

Conclusion

As we've said all along, this book isn't about the best way to have a baby. This book is about the best way for *you* to have a baby. Whether it's a childbirth expert, your mother, your sister, or your best friend, no one can tell you what's best for you better than you can. That's not to say that what anyone has to teach or hand down or share won't be of any help to you. It most certainly was to them, but it is based on who they are and shaped by their own experiences. It will only be of help to *you* if it also fits who you are. You may not know about giving birth, but you do know some very important things about yourself. These are the things that will lead you to filling in the blanks when it comes to the birth that's right for you.

> You may not know about giving birth, but you do know some very important things about yourself. These are the things that will lead you to filling in the blanks when it comes to the birth that's right for you.

Just like any experience in life, you may not have a lot to go on. Life is full of unknowns, and there will always be risk no matter how much control you believe you have. Birth is no different. Just as in life before pregnancy, there are decisions to be made, pieces of advice to sort through, relationships to forge, chances to take, and expectations to be realized or not. As you navigate through this new experience, or an experience you'd like to do differently this time around, run any questions or doubts by the real expert—you. Not everything you come up with will work out perfectly. Life's not perfect. But what matters most is that the answers feel more like your own than anyone else's. In the end, the one person who needs to be able to live with any decision you make about what's best for you, is you.

> No one does it better than anyone else—we do it the best way we know how—just by being ourselves.

As you set out to find what's "best," keep in mind that there will always be new studies, new advances, new childbirth strategies. There is a world of information and research out there to keep you busy for years—and maybe cause you to change your mind a million times over. The irony of it is you'll probably end up finding a study that supports the very thing you wanted in the first place. Or, you might change your mind and end up supporting something because you thought the experts knew better and, when all is said and done, wind up not feeling so great about it. Go with what you feel is right. That can lead you to a birth experience where you feel good about you.

People will always have something to say about whatever you do. Having a cesarean delivery doesn't mean you haven't given birth. Going through a thirty-six-hour labor without medication doesn't make you a crazy person. And you're not any less of a woman if you get the epidural. What's right for you may be completely wrong for your best friend. No one does it better than anyone else—we do it the best way we know how—just by being ourselves.

Having a baby is just bigger than you know, until you have one. But you can find your way through it in any capacity that works for you, whether you consider childbirth a personal journey or you just want to get through the birth part because it's the only way to get to the parent part. What we want for you is what you want for yourself. And whenever you're in doubt about what that is, consult the real expert—you. That's a tool you'll be able to rely on for the rest of your life.

Resources

These resources are not an endorsement or reflection of our personal preferences. They're simply meant to offer some direction should you need it.

Childbirth Education

Association of Labor Assistants & Childbirth Educators (ALACE)
P.O. Box 390436
Cambridge, MA 02139
(888) 222-5223 or (617) 441-2500
www.alace.org

The Bradley Method of Natural Childbirth
P.O. Box 5224
Sherman Oaks, CA 91413-5224
(800) 4-A-BIRTH or (818) 788-6662
www.bradleybirth.com

HypnoBirthing Institute
P.O. Box 810
Epsom, NH 03234
(877) 798-3286
www.hypnobirthing.com

International Childbirth Education Association (ICEA)
P.O. Box 20048
Minneapolis, MN 55420
(952) 854-8600
www.icea.org

Lamaze International
2025 M Street NW, Suite 800
Washington, DC 20036-3309
(202) 367-1128
(800) 368-4404
www.lamaze.org

Practitioners

American College of Nurse-Midwives (ACNM)
8403 Colesville Road, Suite 1550
Silver Spring, MD 20910-6374
(240) 485-1800
www.midwife.org

American College of Obstetricians and Gynecologists (ACOG)
409 12th Street, SW
P.O. Box 96920
Washington, DC 20090-6920
(202) 638-5577
www.acog.org

Midwives Alliance of North America (MANA)
375 Rockbridge Road, Suite 172-313
Lilburn, GA 30047
(888) 923-MANA
www.mana.org

North American Registry of Midwives (NARM)
5257 Rosestone Drive
Lilburn, GA 30047
(888) 842-4784
www.narm.org

Doulas

Doulas of North America (DONA)
P.O. Box 626
Jasper, IN 47547
(888) 788-DONA
www.dona.org

National Association of Postpartum Care Services
800 Detroit Street
Denver, CO 80206
(800) 453-6852
www.napcs.org

See also: Association of Labor Assistants & Childbirth Educators (ALACE) on page 213 and International Childbirth Education Association (ICEA) on page 214.

Birth Centers

Ina May Gaskin and the Farm Midwifery Center
Summertown, TN 38483
(931) 964-2293
www.inamay.com

National Association of Childbearing Centers (NACC)
3123 Gottschall Road
Perkiomenville, PA 18074
(215) 234-8068
www.birthcenters.org

Home Birth

The InterNational Association of Parents & Professionals for Safe Alternatives in Childbirth (NAPSAC)
Route 4, Box 646
Marble Hill, MO 63764
(573) 238-2010
www.napsac.org

See also: Ina May Gaskin and the Farm Midwifery Center on page 215.

Alternative Practitioners

The American Association of Naturopathic Physicians
3201 New Mexico Avenue NW, Suite 350
Washington, DC 20016
(866) 538-2267 or (202) 895-1392
www.naturopathic.org

American Chiropractic Association (ACA)
1701 Clarendon Blvd.
Arlington, VA 22209
(800) 986-4636
www.amerchiro.org

American Herbalists Guild
1931 Gaddis Road
Canton, GA 30115
(770) 751-6021
www.americanherbalistsguild.com

National Certification Commission for Acupuncture
& Oriental Medicine (NCCAOM)
11 Canal Center Plaza, Suite 300
Alexandria,VA 22314
(703) 548-9004
www.nccaom.org

Breast Feeding

La Leche League International
P.O. Box 4079
Schaumburg, IL 60168-4079
(800) LaLeche
www.lalecheleague.org

Postpartum Support

National Mental Health Association
2001 N. Beauregard Street, 12th Floor
Alexandria,VA 22311
(703) 684-7722

National Mental Health Association Resource Center
(800) 969-NMHA
www.nmha.org

Postpartum Support International
927 North Kellogg Avenue
Santa Barbara, CA 93111
(805) 967-7636
www.postpartum.net

Other Resources

Maternity Center Association (MCA)
281 Park Avenue S, 5th Floor
New York, NY 10010
(212) 777-5000
www.maternitywise.org

Waterbirth International
P.O. Box 1400
Wilsonville, Oregon 97070
(800) 641-2229
www.waterbirth.org

Index